GCSE ENGLISH/ENGLISH LITERATURE

Support Book

Joanna Crewe

Series Editor: Peter Buckroyd
Consultant: Julia Waines

OXFORD
UNIVERSITY PRESS

OXFORD
UNIVERSITY PRESS

Great Clarendon Street, Oxford OX2 6DP

Oxford University Press is a department of the University of Oxford.
It furthers the University's objective of excellence in research, scholarship,
and education by publishing worldwide in

Oxford New York

Auckland Bangkok Buenos Aires
Cape Town Chennai Dar es Salaam Delhi Hong Kong Istanbul
Karachi Kolkata Kuala Lumpur Madrid Melbourne Mexico City Mumbai
Nairobi São Paulo Shanghai Taipei Tokyo Toronto

Oxford is a registered trade mark of Oxford University Press
in the UK and in certain other countries

British Library Cataloguing in Publication Data available

ISBN 0 19 832078 7

3 5 7 9 10 8 6 4 2

Typeset by Mike Brain Graphic Design Limited, Oxford

Printed in Italy by Rotolito Lombarda

Acknowledgements

The publisher would like to thank the following for permission to reproduce
photographs:
AXA Sunlife Direct: pp75, 76; BBC Picture Library: p23; BBC Publicity Stills: p98;
Corbis Sygma/RM: p 19; Corbis UK Ltd: pp49, 116; Corbis UK Ltd/Annie Griffiths
Belt: p123; Corbis UK Ltd (Chris Rainier): pp53, 117; Corbis UK Ltd/Kevin
Fleming: p122; Corbis UK Ltd/Jose Luis Pelaez Inc: p84; Corel Professional
Photos: pp13, 36, 93, 104, 121, 125, 126: David Axrell (Artist): p9; Empics: p119;
Getty Images/Stone: pp54, 55; Getty Images/Taxi/Jim Bastardo: p68; Hulton
Picture Library: pp17, 18, 26; Illustrated London News: p33; ImageSource: p50
(left); Ingram Publishing: p101; Kobal Collection/Linda R Chen/Miramax/Buena
Vista: p28; NASA: pp59, 61; Oxford University Press: pp50 (right), 79, 110, 111,
117; Palo Alto: p90; Paul Hunt (Artist): p52; Photodisc : pp50 (centre), 96; Rex
Features/Action Press: p42; Rex Features/Ken McKay: p72; Ronald Grant Archive:
pp6, 7, 10, 15, 20, 81, 106, 107.

We are grateful for permission from the following to include the following
copyright material in this book:
John Agard: lines from 'Half Caste' from *Get Back Pimple* (Viking, 1996),
reprinted by permission of the author c/o Caroline Sheldon Literary Agency, p8;
Sujata Bhatt: lines from 'Search for my Tongue' from *Brunizem* (Carcanet,
1988), reprinted by permission of Carcanet Press Ltd, p15; **Mike Gayle**: extract
from *My Legendary Girlfriend* (1998), reprinted by permission of the publishers,
Hodder & Stoughton Ltd, p120; **William Golding**: extract from *Lord of the Flies*
(1954), reprinted by permission of the publishers, Faber & Faber Ltd, p121;
Barry Hines: extracts from *Kestrel for a Knave* (Michael Joseph, 1968), copyright
© Barry Hines 1968, reprinted by permission of Penguin Books Ltd, pp8, 10, 20;
Tom Leonard: 'Unrelated Incidents' from *Intimate Voices: Selected Works
1965–1983* (Vintage, 1985), reprinted by permission of the author, p23; **Grace
Nichols**: lines from 'Hurricane Hits England' from *Sunrise* (Virago, 1996),
reprinted by permission of Curtis Brown Ltd, London on behalf of Grace
Nichols, p13; **J.B. Priestley**: extracts from *An Inspector Calls* (Heinemann, 1947),
copyright © J B Priestley 1947, reprinted by permission of PFD on behalf of the
Estate of J B Priestley, pp33, 38; **Willy Russell**: extracts from *Our Day Out*
(Methuen, 1984), reprinted by permission of Methuen Publishing Ltd, pp8, 30,
36; **John Steinbeck**: extracts from *Of Mice and Men* (Penguin, 2000), copyright ©
John Steinbeck 1937, 1965, reprinted by permission of Penguin Books Ltd,
pp18, 26; **Quentin Tarantino**: extract from *Pulp Fiction* (1994), reprinted by
permission of the publishers, Faber & Faber Ltd, p28.

and also to the following for their permission:
AXA Sunlife: for Bonus Cashbuilder Plus advertisement, p75; **Dorling
Kindersley**, The Penguin Group for extract from *Eyewitness Travel Guides: New
York* (DK, 1993), p122; **NI Syndication Ltd** for extract from 'Have a Go with
Gord', interview with Tony Gayle by Pat Sheehan, *The Sun*, 27.1.03, p119;
NOISE, an EPSRC funded campaign that aims to raise awareness of science and
engineering among young people, for extract from article about Skateboards,
on their website, www.noisenet.ws, p90.

We regret we have been unable to trace and contact all copyright holders of
material included before publication. If notified the publisher undertakes to
rectify any errors or omissions at the earliest opportunity.

CONTENTS

INTRODUCTION

This book provides Year 10 and 11 students with the skills they need to pass GCSE English and English Literature, or Entry Level English – that means it's for you! That means this book is a non-fiction text, the purposes of which are to inform, explain, and advise. If you're not sure what that means, you need to use this book. Understanding the purpose of a text is just one of the important skills you need to get good grades. This book will help you learn that skill and many more.

There are seven main units in the book, which match up with the seven areas you need to study for your exam and your coursework:

- novels and poems
- drama
- writing original narrative
- non-fiction and media texts
- texts that argue, persuade, and advise
- texts that inform, explain, and describe
- media texts.

In each unit, there are Skills sections and Practice sections. You are given the chance to learn something new in the Skills sections and then have a go at using those skills on your own in the Practice sections. There are questions and activities to help you build your confidence, followed by help so you can check and improve your answers. There are summaries to remind you what you have learned and key points so you remember the essentials. You can also check how much you understand by grading your own skills, before following the advice on what to do next and moving on. At the back of the book there are Quick Practice Activities to do if you want to revise a skill or if you just need some more practice.

Your teacher may pick out certain skills you need to focus on or you may work through the units one by one. However you use this book, it will help you get the best grades you can!

FICTION

As part of your course, you need to show that you have the skills to respond to different types of fiction and to write your own fiction. You need to show:

- how well you understand the **novels and poems** you have studied in the way that you write about them
- how well you understand the **drama** you have studied in the way that you write about it
- how good you are at writing **your own fiction** or original narrative.

You will be tested on some of these skills in the exams. This will involve writing as well as you can about something, without knowing the questions beforehand or being able to discuss them with anyone.

Other skills will be graded from your coursework. This gives you a chance to write about something when you have the time to think carefully and can plan, rewrite, and double-check everything.

This section on fiction will give you all the skills you need, as well as the chance to practise what you have learned, for real success in the exams and with your coursework.

DIFFERENT KINDS OF FICTION

In the first section of this book you will become more familiar with different types of fiction, including narrative, poetry and drama. You will also be looking at different GENRES, or types of narrative.

With ten years of reading experience behind you, you recognise a lot of things about texts without even thinking about it! As an example, look at these three film posters – even if you don't know the film, you can tell straightaway which one is for a horror film, which one is for a fantasy film and which one is for kids.

How could you tell?
Film posters follow certain rules that we all come to recognise. Posters for kids' films always use a lot of colour, have a 'fun' font for the title and very often have images of cute looking animals. Horror film posters usually have a scary image, and dark or red

colours to suggest fear and blood. Fantasy films always show the characters in their strange outfits and some of the magical things they use.

We find it easy to identify these types of posters because we are so used to seeing them follow these rules – and it's the same with texts! We can recognise different types of text because we have seen them so often before.

1 To prove it, match up these descriptions with the extracts below them from different types of text.

Drama script
Layout different from normal text
Names set on the left
Stage directions in brackets or italics

Narrative
Standard prose layout of text
Includes some description
Includes some speech with all correct punctuation

Poetry
Layout different from normal text
Shorter lines
Not necessarily regular sentences, words or punctuation
Includes sound effects, e.g. rhyme or alliteration

MILTON:	How much are the penny chews?
SHOPKEEPER:	Tenpence, the penny chews are tenpence. (She clouts a kid.) Take your 'ands off!
MILTON:	But they're called penny chews.
SHOPKEEPER:	Yes! They're called penny chews but they cost tenpence each.
MILTON:	It's robbery that.

Our Day Out, Willy Russell.

Jud slipped his suit jacket on and flexed his shoulders, smiling at himself in profile through the mirror.
  'Some bird's goin' to be lucky tonight.'
  He fluffed the bob at the front of his hair and walked out whistling.
A Kestrel For a Knave, Barry Hines.

Expain yuself
wha yu mean
when yu say half-caste
yu mean when Picasso
mix red an green
is a half-caste canvas
'Half Caste', John Agard.

Not only can you already identify different types of text, you're already expert at identifying different types of narrative, or genres, too.

2 Match these descriptions of different genre with the extracts below.

Detective stories mention clues, a detective, a crime

Legends mention strange lands, strange creatures, magic

Fictional diaries are written in the first person narrative, in time sequence order, with descriptions of events

Arrows fell among them. One struck Frodo and sprang back. Another pierced Gandalf's hat and stuck there like a black feather. Frodo looked behind. Beyond the fire he saw swarming black figures: there seemed to be hundreds of orcs. They brandished spears and scimitars which shone red as blood in the firelight. *Doom, doom* rolled the drumbeats, growing louder and louder, *doom, doom.*
The Fellowship of the Ring, J.R.R. Tolkein.

Holmes, after a careful examination through the open window, endeavoured in every way to force the shutter open, but without success. There was no slit through which a knife could be passed to raise the bar. Then with his lens he tested the hinges, but they were of solid iron, built firmly into the massive masonry. 'Hum!' said he, scratching his chin in some perplexity, 'my theory certainly presents some difficulties. No one could pass these shutters if they were bolted. Well, we shall see if the inside throws any light upon the matter.'
'The Speckled Band', Sir Arthur Conan Doyle.

Wednesday November 11th
Dr Gray has struck me off his list! He said nipple-swelling is common in boys. Usually they get it when they are twelve and a half. Dr Gray said I was emotionally and physically immature! How can I be immature? I have had a rejection letter from the BBC! And how could I walk to the surgery with swollen nipples?
The Secret Diary of Adrian Mole aged 13¾, Sue Townsend.

As you study and write fiction for your course you will look at many different types of fiction in more detail. Be confident – what you already know about fiction will take you a long way into your course.

PART ONE — CHARACTERS, EVENTS, PREDICTIONS, AND THEMES

YOUR OBJECTIVES ARE . . .

- to listen carefully to a story and talk about the events and characters in it
- to describe what happens and suggest what happens next
- to explain who the characters are and what they do
- to comment on important ideas and themes in the text.

Read this extract from *A Kestrel For A Knave*, by Barry Hines. You may be studying this text for an exam. Billy's big brother Jud has killed Kes, Billy's bird. Kes was a kestrel or type of hawk. Jud was angry because Billy failed to put a bet on for him which would have won him some money. Billy has just found the dead body of his bird and is very upset.

He opened one wing like a fan and on the underside of it, slowly drew a finger down the primaries, down to the body, as though the wing was a feathered instrument, its note too soft for human hearing. He refolded the wing carefully across its back,

5   then carried it through to the living room.

Jud was standing with his back to the fire. His mother was standing at the table, pouring tea. The comic was still on the floor.

'Look what he's done to it, mam! Look at it!'

He held the hawk out to her across the table, yellow legs

10 upwards, jesses dangling, its claws hooks in the air.

'I know, it's a shame, love: but I don't want it.'

She sat down, bringing her face on a level with the hawk.

'Look at it, though! Look what he's done!'

15 She looked at it, curling her top lip, then turned to Jud.

'It wa' a rotten trick, Jud.'

'It wa' a rotten trick what he did, wasn't it?'

20 'I know, but you know how much he thought about that bird.'

'He didn't think half as much about it as I did

25 about that ten quid.'

'He thought world on it though. Take it away from t'table then, Billy.'

'It wasn't worth ten quid was it?'

'I know, but it wa' a rotten trick all t'same. Take it away from
30 my face then, Billy, I've seen it.'

Billy tried to get close to her with the bird, but she wouldn't let him.

'It's not fair on him, mam! It's not fair.'

'I know it's not, but it's done now so there's nowt we can do
35 about it is there?'

'What about him though? What you goin' to do to him? I want you to do summat to him.'

'What can I do?'

'Hit him! Gi' him a good hiding! Gi' him some fist!'

40 Jud snorted and turned round to look at himself in the mirror above the mantelpiece.

NOW TRY THESE QUESTIONS . . .

1 Choose the best description of what happens in this extract.
  a Billy wants his brother to buy him a new bird.
  b Billy wants his mother to understand how upset he is and to punish his brother.
  c Jud wants Billy to sell the bird to get him his ten pounds back.

2 Billy is upset that his brother seems to be getting away with what he's done. Which quote from the extract do you think best shows this?
  a 'Look what he's done, mam. Look at it!'
  b 'Gi' him a good hiding!'
  c 'You never do owt to him!'

3 If you had to pick one word that summarised Billy's feelings in this extract, which of the words on the right would NOT fit?

outrage
tiredness
sadness hatred
ANGER

4 What do you think is most likely to happen after this scene?
  a Billy goes off to bed to cry about the loss of his bird.
  b Billy's mum goes out to buy him a new bird.
  c Jud apologises to Billy for what he has done.
  d Billy storms out of the house in a rage.

Can you explain your choice?

5 Billy is often unfairly treated in his life. This extract is a good example. Even if you don't know the story, which of the following events from *A Kestrel for a Knave* would NOT be a good example of this?

a Billy is picked on by his PE teacher because he can't afford the correct school PE kit.

b Billy's English teacher comes to watch him fly his hawk and praises his skill.

c Billy falls asleep in assembly because he has to get up so early to work before school. He is punished for falling asleep.

AFTER ANSWERING . . .

Read the notes below to help you think about what you have learned.

The first three questions look at how well you've understood what is happening and how the characters feel. As readers we can understand how upset Billy would feel because of the reactions of his mother and brother.

The fourth question looks at suggesting, or predicting, how the characters would act. When you understand the characters, it is obvious that Jud and Billy's mum would not suddenly feel sorry for Billy.

The fifth question asks you to comment on ideas and themes that run all through the story. Once you understand that Billy is often badly treated by the adults in the story, it is easy to see which events fit this theme and which don't.

SUMMARY

Remember to:
- think about how the characters would feel in their situations
- think about how the characters might react to events
- spot themes to help you suggest what might happen next.

WHAT NEXT?

If you need more help with these skills, try quick activities 3 and 4 on page 118. If you think you've got it, you'll have the chance to use them more independently in the Practice section on pages 20–22.

PART TWO – USING THE TEXT TO EXPLAIN YOUR VIEWS

YOUR OBJECTIVE IS . . .

■ to use specific features of the text to help explain your views.

Read this extract from the poem, 'Hurricane Hits England', by Grace Nichols. It appears in the 'Different Cultures' section of the AQA *Anthology*. The poem is about a woman who lives in England, away from her tropical home country. A strong storm makes her feel England is connected to her home country.

It took a hurricane to bring her closer
To the landscape.
Half the night she lay awake,
The howling ship of the wind, its gathering rage,
5   Like some dark ancestral spectre
Fearful and reassuring.

Talk to me Huracan
Talk to me Oya
Talk to me Shango
10   And Hattie,
My sweeping back-home cousin.

Tell me why you visit
An English coast?
What is the meaning
15   Of old tongues
Reaping havoc
In new places?

NOW TRY THESE QUESTIONS . . .

1 Which of these phrases from the text shows how loud and violent the storm was?
  a 'bring her closer'
  b 'Half the night'
  c 'howling ship of the wind'

2 Which of these words from the text shows that the storm is frightening in some ways?
  ■ 'Hattie'   ■ 'spectre'   ■ 'cousin'

3 Which of these phrases from the text shows that she is having confusing feelings about the storm?
a 'Fearful and reassuring'
b 'It took a hurricane'
c 'Talk to me Huracan'

4 Which word best fits in this sentence?

We can see that she feels closely connected to the storm when she calls it, '...............'.

- 'Oya'   • 'ship'   • 'cousin'

5 Which phrase best fits in this sentence?

The poet shows she is talking to the storm as if it were a real person when she says, '...............'.

- 'gathering rage'   • 'Tell me'   • 'English coast'

AFTER ANSWERING . . .

Read the notes below to help you think about what you have learned.

Each question asks you to identify the part of the text that matches the meaning you are searching for. For example, in Question 1, the phrase 'bring her closer' says nothing about loud noise or violence. You need to choose a different phrase.

The third question is more complicated and asks you to think about feeling or emotion words.

The fourth and fifth questions ask you to look for quotes to provide proof for something. This is the heart of the skill you must learn. Do the words you have chosen prove the point?

SUMMARY

Remember to:
- find the part of the text which best shows the view you want to explain
- use your quotes in a sentence.

WHAT NEXT?

If you need more help with these skills, try quick activities 5 and 8 on pages 119–120. If you think you've got it, you'll have the chance to use them more independently in many of the Practice sections.

PART THREE – LOOKING AT LANGUAGE AND STRUCTURE

YOUR OBJECTIVES ARE . . .

■ to identify some features of language
■ to identify some features of structure.

This means being able to comment on the words used in a text and on the way the text has been put together.

Read this extract from the poem, 'Search For My Tongue', by Sujata Bhatt. It appears in the 'Different Cultures' section of the AQA *Anthology*. This poem is about a woman who lives in Britain and speaks English all day. However, her native language, or 'mother tongue', is Gujerati. She is afraid she'll forget how to speak Gujerati if she does not use it.

> And if you lived in a place you had to
> Speak a foreign tongue,
> Your mother tongue would rot,
> Rot and die in your mouth
> 5 Until you had to spit it out.
> I thought I spit it out
> But overnight while I dream
>
> મને હતું કે આખ્ખી જીભ આખ્ખી ભાષા,
> (munay hutoo kay aakhee jeebh aakhee bhasha)
>
> 10 મેં થૂંકી નાખી છે.
> (may thoonky nakhi chay)

NOW TRY THESE QUESTIONS . . .

1 Which of these words show that the poet feels the English language is strange to her, even though she speaks it every day?
■ 'mother'   ■ 'foreign'   ■ 'tongue'

2 The poet uses negative words to show that she is worried she'll lose her Gujerati language. Which of these phrases DO NOT have negative connections?
■ 'rot and die'   ■ 'spit it out'   ■ 'while I dream'

3 The poet can still hear and speak Gujerati in her dreams. Apart from just saying that she can, how does the script on the page SHOW you?

4 How does she make us HEAR how different Gujerati is from English? If you're not sure, read the words out loud.

5 Later in the poem, the language goes back to English. The poet talks about how her mother tongue 'blossoms' out of her mouth.
   a Why do you think the poet chooses to put some Gujerati script right in the middle of the English?
   b Why do you think, after all the negative words about her language dying, she uses the word 'blossoms'?

AFTER ANSWERING . . .

These are some of the hardest skills to grasp, so it may have taken you a while to tackle the questions. Read the notes below to help you think about what you have learned.

The first two questions ask you to look at how the poet selects language. She wants to show that she worries about losing her Gujerati and so uses negative ideas to show her fears.

The third question is more complicated and asks you to look at the structure of the poem. In this case, structure means how it is put together and set out on the page.

The fourth question looks again at language, but focuses more on sound. We can HEAR what Gujerati sounds like by reading out the strange looking words in brackets. It is easy to hear how different it is from English and this is exactly what the poet wanted. Why did she give the sound translation as well as the original script? Because not everyone knows how to read and say the original Gujerati.

The fifth question looks at two areas. The first part is about structure and the second part is about language.

SUMMARY

Remember to:
■ look closely at specific words and phrases
■ look closely at how the text is organised or structured
■ decide what the writer is trying to tell you with the language and structure.

WHAT NEXT?

You'll have the chance to use these skills more independently in the Practice section on pages 23–25.

PART FOUR – SOCIAL, HISTORICAL, AND LITERARY SETTINGS

YOUR OBJECTIVES ARE . . .

- to show you understand how the historical setting has an effect on the text
- to show you understand how the social and cultural setting has an effect on the text
- to show you understand about the literary traditions the text follows

The time and place in which a text was written will usually have an effect on what it includes.

Many of Shakespeare's plays are examples of how the **historical setting** affects a text. Shakespeare made a lot of money from the royals of the time – so he wrote lots of plays that made kings and queens look strong, good, and interesting.

The effects of **social and cultural effects** can be seen in most texts, depending on the time in which they were written. For example, many Victorian stories show their female characters as weak and silly, as women then had a very different role from women today.

After the Sherlock Holmes stories first came out and were very popular, lots of detective stories soon followed. These can be said to follow in the **literary tradition** of detective stories.

If you can comment on any of these three types of setting when talking about texts, you will gain extra marks.

Read the extract on the next page, which is taken from *Of Mice and Men*, by John Steinbeck. This novel was written in America in the 1930s, when many people were very poor. They had to travel around looking for work to earn enough to stay alive. This was a shock in a country where people were used to making money and buying their own land. Women had few chances in life, apart from being married and having a family. They were often thought of as possessions of their husbands or fathers. Black Americans had a daily struggle with strong prejudice against them because of their colour. They were not treated as equal by most white Americans.

Curley's father owns the ranch where Lennie and his friend George, who looks after him, work. Lennie has disobeyed George and accidentally killed the puppy he was given. At this point, Lennie is interrupted in the barn by Curley's wife.

Curley's wife came around the end of the last stall. She came very quietly, so that Lennie didn't see her. She wore her bright cotton dress and the mules with the red ostrich feathers. Her face was made up and the little sausage curls were all in place. She was
5 quite near to him before Lennie looked up and saw her.

In a panic he shovelled hay over the puppy with his fingers. He looked sullenly up at her.

She said, 'What you got there, sonny boy?'

Lennie glared at her. 'George says I ain't to have nothing to do
10 with you — talk to you or anything.'

She laughed. 'George giving you orders about everything?'

Lennie looked down at the hay. 'Says I can't tend no rabbits if I talk to you or anything'. She said quietly,
15 'He's scared Curley'll get mad. Well, Curley got his arm in a sling — an' if Curley gets tough, you can break his other han'. You didn't put nothing
20 over on me about getting it caught on no machine.'

But Lennie was not to be drawn. 'No, sir. I ain't gonna
25 talk to you or nothing.'

She knelt in the hay beside him. 'Listen,' she said. 'All the guys got a horse-shoe tenement* going on. It's on'y about four o'clock. None of them guys is goin' to leave that tenement. Why
30 can't I talk to you? I never get to talk to nobody. I get awful lonely.'

Lennie said, 'Well, I ain't supposed to talk to you or nothing.'

'I get lonely,' she said. 'You can talk to people, but I can't talk to nobody but Curley. Else he gets mad. How'd you like not to talk
35 to anybody?'

Lennie said, 'Well, I ain't supposed to. George's scared I'll get into trouble.'

*Glossary: tenement = competition.

FICTION

NOW TRY THIS ACTIVITY . . .

Two of the quotes below tell you something about the position of women in this society. The other two tell you how important it was not to lose your job.

1 Decide which quotes tell you which things.

2 Describe how each quote makes its point.

> She said quietly, 'He's scared Curley'll get mad'.

> 'I can't talk to nobody but Curley. Else he gets mad.'

> 'I get awful lonely.'

> 'George says I ain't to have nothing to do with you – talk to you or anything.'

AFTER ANSWERING . . .

If you can answer the questions above correctly, you can use a text to make a point about the social and historical setting, and you have achieved your objective. Read the notes below to help you think about what you have learned.

What do the quotes tell you about how Curley treats his wife? He can treat her like this because of the position of women in this society. What was the position of women?

What was the position of the workers, in a society where jobs and money were hard to come by? How does this make Lennie feel and act?

SUMMARY

Remember to:

■ think about the time and place in which the text was written

■ decide if the ideas from those times and places have affected what happens in the text.

WHAT NEXT?

If you need more help with these skills, try quick activity 5 on page 118. If you think you've got it, you'll have the chance to use them more independently in the Practice section on pages 26–27.

PRACTICE – CHARACTERS, EVENTS, PREDICTIONS, AND THEMES

REMEMBER: the key is to think about the themes in the text and how the characters might feel and react.

Read the following extract from *A Kestrel For A Knave*, by Barry Hines. You may be studying this text for an exam. This extract comes from early in the novel. Billy was up early to do his paper round and is now in registration. He is daydreaming about his kestrel.

Anderson?	Sir!	/
Armitage?	Yes Sir!	/
Bridges?	Away Sir!	O
Casper?	Yes Sir?	/
Ellis?	Here Sir!	/
Fisher?	German Bight.	/

5

Mr Crossley dug the biro point in. Too late, the black stroke skidded diagonally down the square. He lifted his face slowly to the class. All the boys were looking at Billy.

10 'What was that?'
'It was Casper, Sir.'
'Did you say something, Casper?'
'Yes Sir, I didn't . . .'
'Stand up!'

15 Billy stood up, red. The boys looked up at him, grinning, lolling back in their chairs in anticipation.
'Now then, Casper, what did you say?'
'German Bight, Sir.'
The rest of the class laughed out, some screwing their fore
20 fingers into their temples and twitching their heads at Billy.
'He's crackers, Sir!'
'He can't help it.'
'SILENCE.'
There was silence.

25 'Is this your feeble idea of a joke, Casper?'
'No, Sir.'
'Well what was the idea then?'
'I don't know, Sir. It wa' when you said Fisher. It just came out, Fisher – German Bight. It's the shipping forecast, Sir; German

30   Bight comes after Fisher; Fisher, German Bight, Cromarty. I know
      'em all, I listen to it every night, I like to hear the names.'
          'And so you thought you'd enlighten me and the class with your
      idiotic information?'
          'No, Sir.'
35   'Blurting out and making a mess of my register.'
          'It just came out, Sir.'
          'And so did you, Casper. Just came out from under a stone.'
          The class roared out again, tossing their heads back and scraping
      their chairs, banging their desk lids ands thumping the backs and
40   arms of any boy in range, using the joke as a mere excuse to cause
      havoc.
          'Quiet! I said QUIET.'

NOW PRACTISE . . .

Getting started

These first two questions ask you to explain who the characters in
the text are and what they do.

1 Explain how Mr Crossley reacts to Billy's accidental outburst.
Use at least one of the following suitable quotes in your answer.
'making a mess of my register'
'idiotic information'
'Just came out from under a stone'

Use the question to help you phrase your answer. For example,

> Mr Crossley reacts .... to Billy's outburst. This is
> shown when he says, '....................' because he is suggesting
> that ....

2 Explain how Billy reacts to the reaction of his classmates. Use
the following quote in your answer.
'Billy stood up, red.'

The next step . . .

The next two questions on page 22 ask you to make predictions
about the characters using what you have learned about them
from the extract. Use the following structure to help you answer
Question 3.

> I think Mr Crossley would .... because ....
> He proves this when he says '....................,' because it shows his
> feelings of .... towards Billy.

3 Make a prediction about Mr Crossley. Do you think he would ever help Billy? If not, why not? Use quotes in your answer to prove what you are saying.

4 Do you think that the rest of Billy's classmates are good friends of his, or not? Use quotes in your answer to prove what you are saying.

The final step . . .

5 This last question practises the hardest skill to master – turning what you have recognised about the themes and ideas into a full answer. Look for what happens in the story, then search for words and phrases that back up what you are trying to say. Quote these examples in your answer, like this model:

> We can see that this is an example of Billy being treated badly by adults because Mr Crossley lets the other boys in the class ....

AFTER ANSWERING . . .

If you have completed all these questions, you can begin to feel confident about your skills with these objectives. Look at the checklist below and grade your skills to make sure you are ready to tackle an exam-level question.

Skill	I need more practice	I usually get it right	I am ready to move on
Talk about events and characters			
Describe what happens and predict what will happen next			
Explain who characters are and what they do			
Comment on important themes and ideas			
Refer closely to the text in my answers			

PRACTICE – LOOKING AT LANGUAGE AND STRUCTURE

REMEMBER: the key is to think about how words are used and how the text has been organised.

Read this extract from the poem, 'Unrelated Incidents', by Tom Leonard. It is taken from the AQA *Anthology*.

this is thi
six a clock
news thi
man said n
5   thi reason
a talk wia
BBC accent
iz coz yi
widny wahnt
10 mi ti talk
aboot thi
trooth wia
voice lik
wanna yoo
15 scruff. if
a toktaboot
thi trooth
lik wanna yoo
scruff yi
20 widny thingk
it wuz troo.
jist wanna yoo
scruff tokn.
thirza right
25 way ti spell
ana right way
ti tok it. this
is me tokn yir
right way a
30 spellin. this

is ma trooth
yooz doant no
thi trooth
yirsellz cawz
35 yi canny talk
right. This is
the six a clock
nyooz. belt up.

NOW PRACTISE . . .

Getting started

The first three questions ask you to look at the language used in the poem and the effect of the sound of the words the poet has chosen.

1 Read the extract out loud a few times. It will help you a lot if you think of a Scottish accent while you are reading. What do you notice about how the poem sounds? Explain how the strange spelling of the words helps you to say them out loud in the way the poet wants you to say them. For example,

> By spelling the words differently to normal, the poet makes them sound .... The word '..........' is one example of this.

2 Why does the poet talk about sounding like 'wonna yoo scruff'? What is he trying to say about people who are 'scruffs'? Use the question to help you phrase your answer. For example,

> The poet talks about sounding like a 'scruff' because he is saying he ....

3 What is the poet saying about how people who read the news on radio or television sound? Use one of the following suitable quotes in your answer, but make sure you explain how it helps back up what you mean.

BBC accent

yi widny thingk it wuz troo

ana right way ti tok it

4 Which words from the extract could you use to explain the poet's mood? First, decide if he seems happy, angry or sad. Then choose three of the following five phrases to help explain his mood in a full answer.

yi widny wahnt

'ma trooth

belt up

yi canny talk right

yooz doant no thi trooth yirsellz

Use the following structure to help you answer the question.

> The poet shows that he is feeling .... when he says '..........',
> which means that he thinks .... He says that '..........',
> showing that he feels ....

The next step . . .

This next question asks you to look at the structure of the poem. Remember, the best answers try to link the structure of a text to the message the writer is trying to give.

5 The poem is set out as it is for a specific purpose. Choose from the reasons below why you think this is. Now add more explanation to turn your chosen reason into a full written answer. Explain how the way the poem is set out fits with what the poet is trying to say.

- It's easier to read
- It looks like a newsreader's autocue
- He wanted to make it look longer

The final step . . .

This final question asks you to put all your information about this poem together.

6 Write a long answer to the question below. Don't forget to use quotes in your answer.

How does the language and structure used in this poem help to convey the poet's message about accents?

AFTER ANSWERING . . .

If you have completed all these questions, you can begin to feel confident about your skills with these objectives. Look at the checklist below and grade your skills to make sure you are ready to tackle an exam-level question.

Skill	I need more practice	I usually get it right	I am ready to move on
Identify some features of language			
Identify some features of structure			
Refer closely to the text in my answers			

PRACTICE – SOCIAL, HISTORICAL, AND LITERARY SETTINGS

REMEMBER: the key is to think about how the social, cultural and historical setting and literary traditions might affect the text.

Read this extract from *Of Mice and Men*, by John Steinbeck. At this point in the story, Lennie, the simple ranch worker, has gone to talk to Crooks, the black stable hand, in Crooks' room.

Crooks leaned forward over the edge of the bunk. 'I ain't a southern negro,' he said. 'I was born right here in California. My old man had a chicken ranch, 'bout ten acres. The white kids came to play at our place, an' sometimes I went to play with them, and
5   some of them was pretty nice. My ol' man didn't like that. I never knew till long later why he didn't like that. But I know now.' He hesitated, and when he spoke again his voice was softer. 'There wasn't another coloured family for miles around. And now there ain't a coloured man on this ranch an' there's jus' one family in
10 Soledad.' He laughed. 'If I say something, why it's just a nigger sayin' it.'
     Lennie asked, 'How long you think it'll be before them pups will be old enough to pet?'
     Crooks laughed again. 'A guy can talk to you an' be sure you
15 won't go blabbin'. Couple of weeks an' them pups'll be alright. George knows what he's about. Jus' talks, an' you don't understand nothing.' He leaned forward excitedly. 'This is just a nigger talkin', an' a busted-back nigger. So it don't mean nothing, see? You couldn't remember it, anyways. I seen it over an' over an'
20 over – a guy talkin' to another guy and it don't make no difference if he don't hear or understand. The thing is, they're talkin', or they're settin' still not talkin'. It don't make no difference, no difference.' His excitement had increased until he pounded his knee with his hand. 'George can tell you screwy things, and it
25 don't matter. It's just the bein' with another guy. That's all.'

NOW PRACTISE . . .

All of the following questions ask you to think about how the historical and social setting of this story affects what the characters do, think and say. You have to include what you know about the setting in your answers.

1 Why didn't Crooks' father like him playing with the white kids as a child? Use your understanding of the way black people were treated in America at this time to help you explain. For example,

In 1930s America, ...

2 Which one word in this extract is a huge clue to the attitudes towards black people that Crooks has to live with? Explain how the use of this word is very different today. For example,

The word '..........' is used by Crooks to describe himself, but nowadays ....

3 Crooks has a very different position in society from the white men on the ranch. Explain how it is different. Use one of the following suitable quotes to help you explain.

'If I say something, why it's just a nigger saying it.'

'it don't mean nothing'

'I never knew till long later why he didn't like that.'

4 How do you know that Crooks is angry about the way he is treated? Use either something Crooks says or something he does to back up your answer. For example,

You get the feeling that Crooks is angry about the way he is treated because ....

AFTER ANSWERING . . .

If you have completed all these questions, you can begin to feel confident about your skills with these objectives. Look at the checklist below and grade your skills to make sure you are ready to go on.

Skill	I need more practice	I usually get it right	I am ready to move on
Talk about the historical setting and its effects			
Talk about the social and cultural setting and its effects			
Talk about the literary traditions			
Refer closely to the text in my answers			

PART ONE – RESPONDING TO DRAMA TEXTS

YOUR OBJECTIVES ARE . . .

- to make a personal response to a play
- to explain and give reasons for your views.

Read this short extract from the script for the film *Pulp Fiction*, by Quentin Tarantino. The two characters are hitmen, who have stopped at a diner for food just after committing a murder. Jules is explaining why he won't eat pork.

	VINCENT:	Want a sausage?
	JULES:	Naw, I don't eat pork.
	VINCENT:	Are you Jewish?
5	JULES:	I ain't Jewish, man, I just don't dig on swine.
	VINCENT:	Why not?
	JULES:	They're filthy animals. I don't eat filthy animals.
10	VINCENT:	Sausages taste good. Pork chops taste good.
15	JULES:	A sewer rat may taste like pumpkin pie. I'll never know 'cause even if it did I wouldn't eat it. Pigs sleep and root* in the dirt. That's a filthy animal. I don't wanna eat nothin' that ain't got enough sense to disregard its own faeces.
	VINCENT:	How about dogs? Dogs eat their own faeces.
	JULES:	I don't eat dog either.
20	VINCENT:	Yes, but do you consider a dog to be a filthy animal?
	JULES:	I wouldn't go so far as to call a dog filthy, but they're definitely dirty. But a dog's got personality. And personality goes a long way.
25	VINCENT:	So by that reasoning if a pig had a better personality, he'd cease to be a filthy animal?
	JULES:	We'd have to be talkin' 'bout one charmin' pig. It'd have to be the Cary Grant* of pigs.

*Glossary: root = dig; Cary Grant = 1950/60s film star known for charm.

It is important that you can show WHAT you think of a play. However, it is even more important to say WHY you feel that way. For example, when you write about what Jules and Vincent are discussing here, you might say,

I thought that the conversation between Jules and Vincent was funny.

To improve this answer, you would need to add more. For example,

I thought it was funny because you do not expect gangsters to be so picky about what they eat. It seems a strange conversation to have just after they've committed murder.

NOW TRY THIS ACTIVITY . . .

Now you need to try this skill of giving reasons for your views. Complete the following sentence, adding a clear reason. You may decide to focus on something about the characters, what they say, or maybe some of the words they use.

I did/did not like this extract from the film because ....

AFTER ANSWERING . . .

It's important to remember why you are asked to explain your opinions. It doesn't matter if you like or dislike something, but you must explain WHY you have made that choice. They are looking to see if you can give good reasons for your opinions and if your reasons show that you properly understand the play.

SUMMARY

Remember to:
- decide what you think about the play
- write about the reasons for your views
- find the part of the play which best shows the view you want to explain
- use your quotes in a sentence.

WHAT NEXT?

If you need more help with these skills, try quick activities 5 and 7–9 on pages 119–121. If you think you've got it, you'll have the chance to use them more independently in the Practice sections on pages 36–39.

PART TWO – STRUCTURE AND CHARACTER

- to show you understand how plays are structured
- to recognise how characters are revealed through what they do and say
- to refer to specific features in the play to help explain your views.

This means looking at the way a play is organised and identifying how that affects the meaning of the play.

Read this extract from *Our Day Out*, by Willy Russell. You may be studying this play for a piece of coursework. This extract comes from near the beginning of the play. Mrs Kay is taking her Progress Class on a school trip, but Mr Briggs wants to stop them going and has gone to see the headmaster.

	BRIGGS:	It'll have to be cancelled.
	HEAD:	If it is she'll resign.
	BRIGGS:	Good. The school would be better off without her.
	HEAD:	There's not many of her type about y'know. By and
5		large I reckon she does a good job. She keeps them
		well out of the way with their reading machines and
		plasticine. It's just when she gets let loose with them.
	BRIGGS:	OK. I'll have to go with her, won't I?
		[Blackout HEAD's study as we bring up Mrs Kay talking
10		*to a young teacher, Susan. Around them are lively excited*
		kids in random groups. Two kids are pulling and pushing
		each other.]
	MRS KAY:	Maurice! Come away from that road!
	MAURICE:	I'm sorry, miss.
15	MRS KAY:	Come on, keep on the side where it's safe.
		[Two older kids (fifteen) come rushing out of school and
		approach the teachers.]
	REILLY:	Ey, miss hang on, hang on . . . can we come with y',
		miss. Can we?
20	DIGGA:	Go on, miss, don't be tight, let's come.
	REILLY:	Go on, miss . . . say yeh.
	MRS KAY:	Brian, you know it's a trip for the Progress Class.
	REILLY:	Yeh, well, we used to be in the Progress Class didn't
		we?

25	**SUSAN:**	But Brian, you're not in the Progress Class any longer, are you? Now that you can read and write you're back in normal classes.
	REILLY:	Agh, miss, come on . . .
30	**MRS KAY:**	Brian, you know that I'd willingly take you, but it's not up to me.

NOW TRY THESE QUESTIONS . . .

1 This extract tries to show how very different Mr Briggs and Mrs Kay are. Choose the best point from below to prove this. Try to add a little more information to your chosen point, perhaps with a quote.

   a The playwright has decided to show Mr Briggs and Mrs Kay each in a different place.

   b The playwright has left Mr Briggs inside the school, trying to stop the trip, whereas Mrs Kay is outside, ready to take the children out.

   c The playwright shows that Mrs Kay is very positive and Mr Briggs is very negative about the school trip.

2 Make a prediction about Mr Briggs. Do you think he ever gets to enjoy the trip? If not, why not? Use the following structure to help you and add quotes to prove what you are saying.

> I think Mr Briggs would .... because .... He proves this when he says ' .... ,' because it shows his feelings of .... towards the trip.

3 Do you think that Mrs Kay is liked and respected by the students, or not? Use the question to help you phrase your answer and add quotes to prove what you are saying.

4 By the time the trip sets off, most audiences have begun to like Mrs Kay and dislike Mr Briggs.

How much do you think this extract helps to explain the audience's reactions? Look for things that happen, as well as words and phrases that back up what you are trying to say. Use them as examples. For example,

> We can see that this is an example of two opposing characters being shown in very different lights, because ....

AFTER ANSWERING . . .

Read the notes below to help you think about what you have learned.

You must be able to show that you understand the characters and that you can see the links between some of the dramatic structures used and what the play is trying to say.

The first question asks you to identify what dramatic structures and devices are being used in this extract.

The next two questions ask you to make predictions about the characters using what you have learned about them from the extract.

In the last question, you are asked to turn what you have recognised about the structure and characters into a full answer. You should have noticed that Mr Briggs is made to look mean and miserable next to the positive and likeable Mrs Kay. You must also be able to give specific examples of how the playwright does this.

SUMMARY

Remember to:
- think about how the characters would feel in their situations
- think about how the characters might react to events
- find the part of the play which best shows the view you want to explain
- use your quotes in a sentence.

WHAT NEXT?

If you need more help with these skills, try quick activities 3, 4 and 9 on pages 118–121. If you think you've got it, you'll have the chance to use them more independently in the Practice section on pages 36–37.

PART THREE – LANGUAGE AND CONTEXT

YOUR OBJECTIVES ARE . . .

- to identify the ways in which language is used in a play
- to show you understand how the social and historical context has an effect on the play.

This means understanding the specific meaning of words and phrases, as well as quoting them in your writing about plays.

Read this extract from *An Inspector Calls*, by J.B. Priestley, written in 1945. You may be studying this play for a piece of coursework. This extract comes from near the beginning of the play, which is set in 1912, just before the beginning of the First World War. Birling and his family are discussing politics and Birling is very confident in his opinions.

	BIRLING:	We're in for a time of steadily increasing prosperity.
	GERALD:	I believe you're right, sir.
	ERIC:	What about war?
	BIRLING:	Glad you mentioned it, Eric. I'm coming to that. Just
5		because the Kaiser makes a speech or two, or a few
		German officers have too much to drink and begin
		talking nonsense, you'll hear some
		people say that war's inevitable. And
		to that I say – fiddlesticks! . . .
10	ERIC:	Yes, I know – but still –
	BIRLING:	Just let me finish, Eric. You've a lot to
		learn yet. And I'm talking as a hard-
		headed, practical man of business.
		And I say there isn't a chance of war. The world's
15		developing so fast that it'll make war impossible. Look
		at the progress we're making. In a year or two we'll
		have aeroplanes that will be able to go anywhere. And
		look at the way the auto-mobile's making headway –
		bigger and faster all the time. And then ships. Why, a
20		friend of mine went over this new liner last week – the
		Titanic – she sails next week – forty-six thousand eight
		hundred tons – forty-six thousand eight hundred tons
		– New York in five days – and every luxury – and
		unsinkable, absolutely unsinkable. That's what you've
25		got to keep your eye on, facts like that.

NOW TRY THESE QUESTIONS . . .

1 Gerald says very little, but what one word does he use that shows he respects Birling?

right

believe

sir

2 Eric also respects Birling, who is his father. However, how can we tell Eric does not completely agree with everything his father says? Which statement do you think best shows this?
   a He asks him a question.
   b He uses the word 'but'.
   c He starts talking before Birling has finished.

3 Birling is a confident man, who is very sure of his opinions. Which three words or phrases do you think show his confidence?
   a 'fiddlesticks'
   b 'nonsense'
   c 'man of business'
   d 'impossible'
   e 'absolutely unsinkable'
   f 'isn't a chance'

   Now put your chosen words into a sentence which explains his attitude. For example,

   We can see that Birling is a very self-confident man who believes that he is right, because he uses words such as .... which shows .... He also uses the words .... , which show ....

4 Although Birling is confident in his opinions, his thoughts on war show us that he can be wrong. How do you know this?

5 Birling confidently talks about something else which we know had a very different outcome. What is the other thing he is wrong about?

6 Birling is presented at the start of the play as quite a disagreeable character, who thinks he is always right. How does the extract show this?

AFTER ANSWERING . . . •••

Read the notes below to help you think about what you have learned.

In this section, you must be able to show that you can link the characters' words with what the characters actually mean and that you can also refer to the context.

The first three questions look at how well you understand the importance of some of the language used.

The fourth and fifth questions ask you to think about what you can explain about the context of the play. Remember, although this play was written in 1945, it is set in 1912 just before the First World War.

In the last question you need to put everything you know about the language and context together. It is important to link Birling's superior attitude to the way that he speaks, as well as to the fact that we know he is later proved wrong about a lot of things. The examiners will look to see if you can give specific examples of how the playwright does this.

SUMMARY

Remember to:
- think about which words show what characters really mean
- think about the time and place in which the play was written and set.

WHAT NEXT?

If you need more help with these skills, try quick activities 4 and 9 on pages 118 and 121. If you think you've got it, you'll have the chance to use them more independently in the Practice section on pages 38–39.

PRACTICE – STRUCTURE AND CHARACTER

REMEMBER: the key is to show you understand how a play is structured and how characters are revealed.

Read the following extract from *Our Day Out*, by Willy Russell. Mrs Kay has decided to add an extra visit to the school trip, but Mr Briggs is very unhappy about it.

	BRIGGS:	(*Suddenly noticing that they have turned off the expected route.*) What's this? Where are we going? This isn't . . .
	MRS KAY:	Oh it's alright Mr Briggs. I've checked with the driver, we thought it might be a good idea if we called in at
5		the zoo for an hour. We've got plenty of time.
	BRIGGS:	But, this trip was arranged so that we could visit Conway Castle.
	MRS KAY:	Ooh, we're going there as well. I know you're very fond of ruins. Now listen everyone, as an extra bonus,
10		we've decided to call in here at the zoo.
		(*Cheers.*)
	BRIGGS:	But look, we can't . . .
	MRS KAY:	Now the rest of the staff will be around if you want to know anything about the various animals, although it's
15		not much good asking me because I don't know one monkey from the next . . .
	BRIGGS:	Mrs Kay . . .
	MRS KAY:	(*Ignoring him*) But, Progress Class, we're very lucky today to have Mr Briggs with us, because Mr Briggs is
20		something of an expert in natural history. He's something of a David Bellamy, aren't you, Mr Briggs? So if you want to know more about the animals, ask Mr Briggs. Now come on. Leave your things on the coach.

NOW PRACTISE . . .

Getting started

The first question asks you to show your personal opinion about this extract. Use the question to help you phrase your answer.

1 Why do you think Mrs Kay has decided to add this extra visit to the trip? Why do you think Mr Briggs is so unhappy about it?

The next step . . .

The next three questions ask you to identify what dramatic devices are used. They also ask you to make predictions about the characters using what you have learned about them in the extract. Use the questions to help you phrase your answers.

2 Why has the playwright deliberately not allowed Mr Briggs to finish any of his sentences and always be interrupted by Mrs Kay? What effect does that have?

3 Why does Mrs Kay call Mr Briggs 'an expert' to the children? What might she be trying to do?

4 How do you think Mr Briggs might react to being called 'an expert'?

The final step . . .

This last question practises the hardest skill to master – turning what you think about the structure and characters into a full answer. You may decide to use some of the information from the previous questions. You should also use words and phrases from the play as examples to back up what you want to say.

5 How does this extract help to show that there is a battle of wills going on between Mr Briggs and Mrs Kay? Use this structure to help you.

> This extract from the play shows us that there is battle of wills going on between Mr Briggs and Mrs Kay for several reasons. First, ... As well as this, ... Another reason is that ....

AFTER ANSWERING . . .

If you have completed all these questions, you can begin to feel confident about your skills with these objectives. Look at the checklist below and grade your skills to make sure you are ready to go on.

Skill	I need more practice	I usually get it right	I am ready to move on
Talk about the structure of the play			
Explain what characters say and do			
Refer closely to the text in my answers			

PRACTICE – LANGUAGE AND CONTEXT

REMEMBER: the key is to show you understand the importance of the language, and the social and historical context of a play.

Read this extract from *An Inspector Calls*, by J.B. Priestley. It is a very tense moment in the play. All the Birling family have discovered that they have played a part in the suicide of a girl they all treated thoughtlessly. The Inspector has led them all to see that what they did to her was terrible, because they didn't care about it at the time.

	SHEILA:	I had her turned out of a job. I started it.
	INSPECTOR:	You helped – but didn't start it. (*Rather savagely, to BIRLING*) You started it.
5	BIRLING:	(*Unhappily*) Look, Inspector – I'd give thousands – yes, thousands –
	INSPECTOR:	You're offering the money at the wrong time, Mr Birling. No, I don't think any of you will forget. Well, Eva Smith's gone. You can't do her any more harm. And you can't do her any good now, either.
10		You can't even say 'I'm sorry, Eva Smith.'
	SHEILA:	(*Who is crying quietly*) That's the worst of it.
	INSPECTOR:	But just remember this. One Eva Smith has gone – but there are millions and millions of Eva Smiths
15		and John Smiths still left with us, with their lives, their hopes and fears, their suffering and their chance of happiness, all intertwined with our lives, and what we say and think and do. We don't live alone. We are members of one body. We are responsible for each other. And I tell you that the
20		time will come when, if men will not learn that lesson, then they will be taught it in fire and blood and anguish. Good night.

NOW PRACTISE . . .

Getting started

These first three questions ask you to understand the importance of some of the language used in this extract.

1 How can you tell that the Inspector is kinder to Sheila than he is to Birling? Look at what he says on line 2.

2 Which one key word does Birling use about Eva that shows us he still thinks like a businessman and not like someone who has truly learned to be sorry?

3 The Inspector wants to teach all the Birling family to behave differently towards people in the future. Why do you think he repeats 'You can't . . .' three times in lines 8–10?

The final step . . .

The last two questions practice the hardest skill – applying what you know about the social and historical context of the play to a question.

Think about when this play was written as well as when it was set. If you can't remember, look back at page 33. What important world events happened around those times?

4 In the Inspector's last lines, he talks about people being taught a lesson 'in fire and blood and anguish'. What could the playwright be referring to?

5 Can you think of what the playwright's overall message to his audience might be? You need to refer to ideas about behaviour, responsibility, and your answer to Question 4.

AFTER ANSWERING . . .

If you have completed all these questions, you can begin to feel confident about your skills with these objectives. Look at the checklist below and grade your skills to make sure you are ready to go on.

Skill	I need more practice	I usually get it right	I am ready to move on
Talk about how language is used in a play			
Talk about the social and historical settings and their effects			
Refer closely to the text in my answers			

PART ONE – THINKING ABOUT YOUR READER

YOUR OBJECTIVES ARE . . .

- to create an original piece of writing
- to think about your reader when you are writing.

Remind yourself what it says about genre on pages 7–9. As a reader you know about different types of story and what each includes. Working out what types of story different people or audiences are likely to enjoy is also something you can already do.

As you know, not every type of person likes every type of story. Although it is a general statement, not many grandmas enjoy violent action stories and not many teenage boys enjoy reading long romance novels. Why not? Well, those types of stories don't tend to include subject matter that interests those particular people.

NOW TRY THESE ACTIVITIES . . .

1 Survey what students in your class like. Ask them to name two types of story they enjoy. They can choose two of the following or any other genres they come up with.

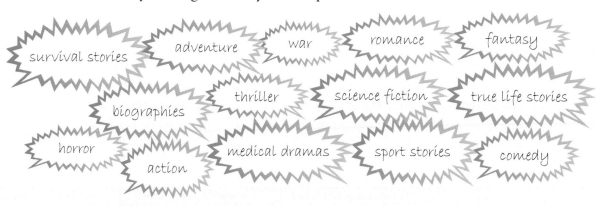

Now look at the results of your survey and the types of people in your class. Can their choices be put into groups? For example,

a Have all the girls tended to go for the same genres?

b What about the boys?

c What about people who are into different interests like rap?

d Are there any genres that appealed to everyone?

You will often find that you can predict quite accurately which groups of people will enjoy certain types of story. You can use this knowledge when choosing a topic for a story of your own.

2 Need more proof that you can pick a story to suit your audience? Use a Venn diagram like this to sort the genres listed in Activity 1. Write each one in the sections according to which genre you think will match which audience.

For example, if you think only teenage girls and grandmas enjoy romance stories, write that genre where those two circles overlap, but not in the circle for adult males. If you think all three groups of people would enjoy comedies, put that in the middle. If you're not sure about any of the genres, discuss it with your class.

Teenage girls   Adult males

Romance

Grandmas

3 Now you have a better idea of what audiences want, you can select ideas for different audiences. Fill in a grid like the one below with your ideas for a genre and a matching story title for each of the audiences. Discuss your ideas with your class.

Audience	Genre	Suggested title
Children under 7		
Women aged 18–40		
Man. United fans		
Teachers		

AFTER ANSWERING . . .

By now, you should have an idea of what specific audiences would be interested in reading. When you begin your own writing, you should have a specific audience in mind so that you know who you are trying to interest. When you make a choice about anything in your story, ask yourself, 'What would my audience enjoy the most?'

SUMMARY

Remember to:
- think about the type of story your reader would like.

WHAT NEXT?

If you need more help with these skills, try quick activity 2 on page 123. If you think you've got it, you'll have the chance to use them more independently in the Practice section on page 49.

PART TWO – ORGANISING YOUR WRITING

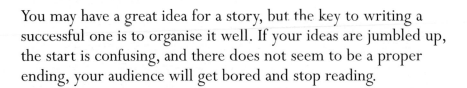

YOUR OBJECTIVES ARE . . .

- to create an original piece of writing
- to organise your writing.

You may have a great idea for a story, but the key to writing a successful one is to organise it well. If your ideas are jumbled up, the start is confusing, and there does not seem to be a proper ending, your audience will get bored and stop reading.

The only way to avoid this is to come up with a plot plan. Plot plans don't have to be long or detailed, but they must put every event in your story into order.

NOW TRY THESE ACTIVITIES . . .

1 Here is a simple plot plan for a story called 'The lucky escape'. Unfortunately it has become muddled up. Put the events into a sensible order. Think carefully about what has to happen first in order for it all to make sense.

- The friends return home, relieved to have escaped any more trouble.
- The friends are just leaving a club when a fight breaks out.
- A group of friends set off on a night out.
- The friends are arrested because they were the only people left at the scene.
- An eye witness comes forward to say the friends were not involved.
- Someone is stabbed to death.

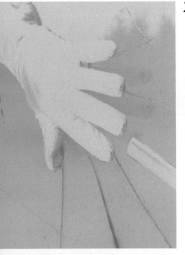

2 Hopefully you have been able to see how events must follow on for the story to make sense. The key for you will be to come up with a plot plan to help you organise your own story.

Think of SIX main sections for a story called 'Tackling a burglar'. You don't need to write a lot about the idea for each section, but they must follow in a sensible order. The first section has been suggested for you, although you could change it for your own.

Tackling a burglar
1 Settling down at 2am for a good night's sleep.
2 ....

3 The most important sections in any story are the opening and the ending. If the opening is boring or too confusing, your audience will stop reading. If the ending is boring or too silly, your audience won't feel very satisfied with your story.

a Plan the opening paragraph for the 'Tackling a burglar' story in more detail. Remember it starts with settling down at 2am. Openings must do certain things, so check off this list to make sure you have included most of the following.

- Briefly introduce the main character.
- Make the scene or situation clear with a description.
- Include an event to get the reader interested.
- Do NOT start with 'Once upon a time' or 'A long time ago.'
- Do NOT bore the reader with long explanations.
- Do NOT confuse the reader by including too many characters.

b Now plan the ending of the same story. Again, make sure you include most of the following.

- Clear up whatever situation has been the subject of the story.
- Still include description to keep the reader interested.
- Include a comment or action from the main character.
- Do NOT write off the main event of the story as a dream or an alien abduction.
- Do NOT be too obvious – the best stories often have surprising endings.
- Do NOT introduce a new character at the last minute.

AFTER ANSWERING . . .

You should now have a good idea of how to organise your story and keep your audience interested.

SUMMARY

Remember to:
- make a plot plan to make sure the events are in a sensible order
- write an opening that introduces the main character and the situation
- make sure your opening grabs the reader's attention
- write an ending that brings the situation in the story to an end
- make sure you have a strong ending.

WHAT NEXT?

If you need more help with these skills, try quick activities 1, 3 and 11 on pages 123, 124 and 128. If you think you've got it, you'll have the chance to use them more independently and start on your own piece of original writing in the Practice section on pages 50–51.

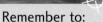

PART THREE – SENTENCES AND PUNCTUATION

YOUR OBJECTIVES ARE . . .

- to create an original piece of writing
- to use basic punctuation with accuracy
- to use some simple and some complex sentences
- to organise sentences into paragraphs.

NOW TRY THESE ACTIVITIES . . .

1 The key to good writing is to check, double check, then check again that the punctuation is correct.

This diagram gives you some simple rules for good punctuation. Gather a selection of books and identify one example of each rule. Copy each example out.

Each sentence has a capital at the start.

Commas either separate lists or show a short pause.

Each sentence has a full stop at the end.

There is some punctuation (e.g. comma, question mark or exclamation mark) BEFORE the close of speech marks.

The names of people or places have capital letters.

Good punctuation

The writing is separated into paragraphs.

There are different paragraphs, e.g. for changes of time, place, point of view, subject or speaker.

Speech is inside speech marks.

All questions have question marks.

Shouting or shocked statements have exclamation marks.

Each new piece of speech from a speaker starts a new line.

If you have ticked each rule, well done – you understand a lot about good punctuation.

2 In the exam, you must use both short simple sentences and long complex ones. It is best if you show that you've chosen to use one or the other type of sentence for a specific purpose. The rules to follow are easy to remember.

Short simple sentences are best used to show shock, fear or suspense in a story, especially after a series of long, drawn out sentences. For example,

Simon froze. or *What was that? A shot?*

Long complex sentences are best used when you want to add description to your writing, because they can help the reader to build up a picture or emotion in their mind. For example,

Simon surveyed the dark, damp room, which was to become his living hell for the next eight days.

or

The sharp sound bounced backwards and forwards across his brain, churning his stomach with terror as he tried to make sense of it.

   a Write two different short simple sentences to show someone's fear at being left alone in a house. Compare your sentences with those of a partner.

   b Now write two long complex sentences to describe a lonely bus station. Try to make one sentence follow on from the other.

3 Paragraphs are essential in a story of your own. They help to organise the story for the reader. The easiest way to arrange your story in paragraphs is to follow your plot plan and begin a new paragraph for each new event. However, here are other reasons to start a new paragraph.

- The place or scene has changed, for example from a shop to a street.
- The time has changed, for example *'Later that night . . .'* or maybe for a flashback.
- The character point of view has changed, for example instead of the hero, we start to see what the villain is thinking.
- A different person has started to speak and the speech marks begin again.

Go through your story plan for 'Tackling a burglar'. How many paragraphs do you think you'll need? Use the list above to check your story when complete.

AFTER ANSWERING . . .

Read the notes below to help you think about what you have learned.

The first activity helps you to check if you have understood the correct use of punctuation.

The second activity shows you how to write short simple sentences and long complex ones.

The last activity helps you to divide your story into paragraphs using a checklist and your plot plan.

SUMMARY

Remember to:
- check and double check your punctuation is correct
- make sure each sentence has one main idea
- use short simple sentences and long complex ones
- organise your story into paragraphs with one new event in each.

WHAT NEXT?

If you need more help with these skills, try quick activities 6 and 7 on pages 126–127. If you think you've got it, you'll have the chance to use them more independently in the Practice section on page 52.

PART FOUR – VOCABULARY AND SPELLING

YOUR OBJECTIVES ARE . . .

- to create an original piece of writing
- to spell words accurately
- to improve the vocabulary you use.

Spelling is another tricky area where it's easy to make mistakes. Get into the habit of checking your own spelling in a dictionary. Take particular care with words you know you have trouble with, as well as with any unfamiliar ones. Refer to the quick activities on page 125 for more hints and tips on spelling.

The vocabulary you use gives you a real chance to make a great impression. Imagine you are an examiner. By the time you have read the words 'nice', 'big', or 'scary' a thousand times, you'd be ready to give good grades to anyone who dares to try something a bit different! So get into the habit of using some powerful descriptive words that really give your reader a sense of who and what you are talking about.

NOW TRY THESE ACTIVITIES . . .

1 Read the following boring opening to a story.

> The <u>old</u> man walked <u>slowly</u> down the <u>big</u> street. He stopped, pushed back his <u>nice</u> hat with his <u>old</u> hand and looked at the <u>scary</u> house in front of him.

Replace the boring words that are underlined with powerful words that suggest this story is in each of the following genres:
a a romance   **b** a horror story   **c** a crime thriller.

You can see that you can get your reader to think about the right images if you choose the right vocabulary.

2 Using extended noun phrases is one of the best ways to add description to any piece of writing. What's an extended noun phrase? A regular noun with extra, descriptive words attached to it. Here are some examples.
'A man' → 'an angry-faced, violent man'
'A forest' → 'a dark, forbidding forest'
'An iron' → 'a heavy blood-stained iron'

FICTION

You can use extended noun phrases to help add description to
scenery, emotions, items or characters. They can help spice up
any sentence in a story. Fill in the gaps in these sentences to add
to the overall effect.

a Avril screamed as the .... woman rushed at her.
b The .... knife lay innocently on the table.
c As the .... crowd roared, the ball flew over his head.
d She had a .... feeling of panic as the door closed.
e He shivered as he entered the .... room.

3 One of the most boring things you can do in a story is to forget
to say HOW a character says something. Make the most of this
chance to add description to your character, the situation and
the speech itself.

Read these sentences which all contain 'said'.
a 'Where have you been?' said Liam.
b 'Isn't it enough?' said Leila.
c Adam said, 'You should have known better.'
d 'You idiot,' said Jaymini, ' that was always the plan.'
e McHenry scowled as he said, 'Why not?'

Now choose one of the other options most suitable to replace
'said' in each sentences.
- wept
- whispered
- screamed
- said with disgust
- spat
- shrieked
- cried
- sighed
- snapped
- snivelled

AFTER ANSWERING . . .

You should now have a better idea of how important spelling and
vocabulary are, and how to improve the vocabulary you use.

SUMMARY

Remember to:
- check your spelling in a dictionary and learn to spell the words
- choose words carefully to make your story more interesting
- use extended noun phrases to add description
- describe how your characters speak.

WHAT NEXT?

If you need more help with these skills, try quick activities 4 and
5 on pages 124–125. If you think you've got it, you'll have the
chance to use them more independently in the Practice section on
page 53.

PRACTICE – THINKING ABOUT YOUR READER

REMEMBER: the key is to think carefully about the type of story your audience would like to read.

When you write a story, your purpose is always to interest and entertain your reader. So you must know who your audience is.

If your audience is a teenage one, you need to think about what types of stories would interest both teenage boys AND girls. You could choose a thriller, a true life story or another genre. The decision is yours. Or, you may discover your audience is another group of people – perhaps young children or older adults. Whoever your audience is, you must think about them even at this early stage of selecting a type of story.

NOW PRACTISE . . .

Work through this list to help you decide on a story and a title.

1 Who is your audience?
2 What types of story would they be interested in?
3 Which of these most interests you yourself?
4 First ideas for a basic story.
5 Final decision on the idea for story.
6 Suggested titles for your story.
7 Final decision on the title.

AFTER ANSWERING . . .

Now you can begin to feel confident about your skills in choosing a story for a particular type of audience. Look at the checklist below and grade your skills to make sure you are ready to plan your story.

Skill	I need more practice	I usually get it right	I am ready to move on
Decide what type of story my audience would like			
Brainstorm ideas for stories			
Brainstorm ideas for titles			
Choose the right story and title for the audience			

PRACTICE – ORGANISING YOUR WRITING

REMEMBER: the key to writing a successful story is good organisation.

The only way to organise your writing well is to make a plot plan. It does not have to be long or detailed, but it must put every event in your story in the right order. So now you have your story idea and your audience in your mind, you need to plan out your plot.

NOW PRACTISE ...

Use a grid like the one opposite to help you structure your story. Fill in your own ideas on the aspects listed in the second column. You may decide to have more or fewer sections, but your plan should follow the same basic order. Keep it simple with just one main event. Perhaps your main character is rather like one of these people – they can be real or imagined.

Sections	Your ideas
The opening	a Briefly introduce the main character. b Make the scene or situation clear to the reader with description.
Build up to the main event	a Build up the tension. b Include description.
The main event: part one	a Make the action interesting with description. b Show the character's emotions and reactions.
The main event: part two	a Make the action interesting with description. b Show the character's emotions and reactions.
The consequences of the main event	a Begin to solve or explain whatever consequences the main event caused. b Keep showing the character's emotions and reactions.
The ending	a Clear up whatever situation has been the subject of the story. b Include a comment or action from the main character. c Remember that the best stories surprise the reader at the end.

AFTER ANSWERING . . .

If you have completed this activity, you can begin to feel confident about your skills in organising your writing. Look at the checklist below and grade your skills to make sure you are ready to build your plan up into your full piece of writing.

Skill	I need more practice	I usually get it right	I am ready to move on
Make a plot plan			
Organise my writing from my plot plan			
Write a good introduction			
Build up tension			
Describe the action			
Describe characters' emotions and feelings			
Write a strong ending			

PRACTICE – SENTENCES AND PUNCTUATION

REMEMBER: the key is to make sure that your punctuation is correct and you organise your sentences and paragraphs well.

NOW PRACTISE . . .

1 Choose a point in your story that you think would benefit from short sentences to add an effect of fear or suspense. Think about whether you want to describe a sound, show a character's emotion, or perhaps make the reader question what is about to happen.

Write a few different short sentences that will create the right effect. First compare your sentences with those of a partner. Then choose the best one to go in your story.

2 Do the same task again, but choose a long complex sentence that will add description in your story.

3 Finally check that you have chosen the right places to start new paragraphs in your story.

AFTER ANSWERING . . .

If you have completed all these questions, you can begin to feel confident about your skills with these objectives. Look at the checklist below and grade your skills to make sure you are ready to move on.

Skill	I need more practice	I usually get it right	I am ready to move on
Use punctuation accurately			
Write short simple sentences			
Write long complex sentences			
Organise sentences into paragraphs			

PRACTICE – VOCABULARY AND SPELLING

PRACTISE SKILLS FROM PART FOUR

REMEMBER: the key is to check your own spelling and to choose descriptive words to add interest.

This extract is taken from *Superman and Paula Brown's New Snowsuit*, by Sylvia Plath, one of the short stories in the AQA *Anthology*. To build up a picture for the reader, the poet uses interesting words to add to the description of her dreams.

These nightly adventures in space began when Superman started invading my dreams and teaching me how to fly. He used to come roaring by in his shiny blue suit with his cape whistling in the wind, looking remarkably like my Uncle Frank who was living with Mother and me. In the magic whirring of his cape I could hear the wings of a hundred sea-gulls, the motors of a thousand planes.

NOW PRACTISE . . .

Re-read the extract. It works so well because the descriptive words help you to see and hear what the poet sees and hears.

1 List all the words and phrases to do with sound. Make a separate list of the words and phrases to do with sight or images. What effects do each of these sets of words have?

2 Think about the words you could choose to improve your own story. Start with words to describe sights and sounds. Then think about the words you explored on pages 47–48.

AFTER ANSWERING . . .

Look at the checklist below and grade your skills.

Skill	I need more practice	I usually get it right	I am ready to move on
Spell words correctly			
Use powerful descriptive words			
Use extended noun phrases			
Describe how characters speak			

Non-fiction

As part of your course, you need to show that you have the skills to respond to different types of non-fiction text. You need to show:

- how well you understand the **non-fiction texts** you have studied in the way that you write about them
- how good you are at writing your own non-fiction texts.

This section on non-fiction is split into four units and cover all the types of text you will need to know about:

- non-fiction and media texts
- texts that argue, persuade, and advise
- texts that inform, explain, and describe
- media texts.

You will be tested on some of these skills in the exams. This will involve writing as well as you can about something, without knowing the questions beforehand or being able to discuss them with anyone.

Other skills will be graded from your coursework. This gives you a chance to write about something when you have the time to think carefully and can plan, rewrite, and double-check everything.

This section on non-fiction will give you all the skills you need, as well as the chance to practise what you have learned, for real success in the exams and with your coursework.

DIFFERENT KINDS OF NON-FICTION

In this section of the book you will become more familiar with all the different types of non-fiction we see around us every day. Non-fiction is not a made-up story, but is writing connected to fact – that's something that can be proved or disproved.

You have ten years of reading experience behind you, so you already recognise a lot of things about non-fiction texts without even thinking about it! The key thing when working with non-fiction is to think about PURPOSE. That means thinking about WHY something has been written.

A writer of non-fiction might choose one or more out of many possible purposes. They might choose from the following purposes.

To ARGUE – to discuss two or more sides of an opinion before coming to a decision.

To PERSUADE – to convince you to think or to do something.

To ADVISE – to give you help or advice about something.

To INFORM – to give you information about something.

To EXPLAIN – to give you reasons for something.

To DESCRIBE – to give you details on what something is like.

Every single non-fiction text, whatever it may be, has at least one specific purpose – even a bus ticket! What's the purpose of a bus ticket? To inform the reader of where you are going and how much you paid.

1 Just to test that out, look around your classroom and in your bag. Find three different non-fiction texts. Remember, you are looking for texts that are connected to fact. You might choose a poster, someone's work on the wall, a homework diary, even a magazine article or advertisement – it's up to you.

What is the purpose, or purposes, of each of them? Look at the description of each of the purposes above – which one seems to fit the best?

2 Below are six different extracts from six different types of texts. Each of them has one main purpose, although you may think some have other purposes too.

Try to match each extract up to the following purposes. If you're not sure, think about what the writer of each one is trying to do and select the purpose that seems the closest.

Discuss what you think with the class afterwards to see if you all agree.

Before travelling to the tropics, it is advisable to visit your doctor to receive the correct inoculations against any diseases for that country.

Although some people believe Sean Connery was the greatest James Bond, many cinema-goers have now come to see Pierce Brosnan as the best Bond actor.

We are working on our water mains in your area to improve our service. As a result of this, you may notice a loss of water supply to your property on the 15th and 16th of January.

As soon as we got here, we all rushed to the fantastic pool in the middle of the complex. As well as an amazing view, it has a cocktail bar in the middle and gets plenty of hot sunshine all day!

The 10.04 train from York to London Kings Cross is delayed by 45 minutes. Refreshments are currently available in the Green Apple Café on Platform 2.

The Super Styler Hair System will make a huge difference to your life and is available for the amazing price of just £24.99. You can't afford to miss out!

In your course you will look in more detail at many different types of non-fiction. Remember, whether you are reading non-fiction or writing it, to think about the PURPOSE of the text – that way you have a better idea of what it should include.
Be confident – what you already know about different types of non-fiction texts will take you a long way into your course. Don't forget to think . . . 'PURPOSE?'

PART ONE – FACT, OPINIONS, AND PRESENTATION

YOUR OBJECTIVES ARE . . .

- to tell the difference between fact and opinion
- to read and understand non-fiction texts
- to recognise the effects of different ways of presenting information.

Usually it is easy to tell a fact, which is something we can prove, from an opinion, which is just what someone believes. Which of these are facts and which are opinions?

a Manchester is in England.
b More people prefer pizzas to burgers.
c Blackburn Rovers is the greatest football team in the world.
d MacDonalds first opened in America.
e Elvis Presley died in 1977.
f Tea is better with two sugars.
g Playing football is a better career than being a doctor.
h Eminem is the best rap star.
i David Beckham has sons called Brooklyn and Romeo.
j Teenagers nowadays get too much pocket money.

However, when a writer wants you to agree with what is in a text, they may make opinions LOOK like facts. For example, in adverts for washing powder all manufacturers will tell you theirs is the best for getting stains out and keeping whites white. Are they ALL right? No – but they want you to think they are, so they make their opinions SOUND like facts.

Now read this article and then have a go at the questions on pages 60–61.

Did We Really Land on the Moon?

ON FEBRUARY 15, 2001, A TELEVISION SHOW TITLED 'CONSPIRACY THEORY: DID WE LAND ON THE MOON?' WAS AIRED IN AMERICA. IT CLAIMED THAT THE MOON LANDINGS THAT TOOK PLACE BETWEEN 1969 AND 1972 WERE ALL AN ELABORATE HOAX, AND THAT MAN NEVER REALLY SET FOOT ON THE MOON.

This programme made you start to wonder about **the truth**. After all, moon landings do not seem to be possible now, so how were they in the 1960s? Did NASA really set out to **fool** billions of people around the world?

The programme showed a lot of NASA photographs with strange images that made you start to question the whole idea of a moon landing. They support the theory that the moon landing was set up by NASA on a sound stage in a secret location in the USA, and **not in space**.

One of the pieces of evidence the programme came up with was very surprising. It pointed out that if you look at any of the NASA photos from the landing, you will notice there are **no** stars in the sky. In fact, you will **never** see any stars in any NASA Moon photographs. **Surely this can't be right?**

Many more questions were raised by the programme, such as:

- **How** could the flag wave on the moon when there was no air or wind to make it?
- **Why** wasn't there a huge blast crater under the landing site of the module as you would expect?
- **Why** did objects in shadow appear as if they had been lit by a second light source, when there should only be the Sun to give out light? Does this suggest there were studio lights?
- The Earth is surrounded by radiation, called the Van Allen Belt. How did the astronauts survive this deadly situation? **Or did they just not go?**

Although the US government and NASA deny any sort of trickery or hoax, one has to consider **why** they might have done such a thing. For money? To cover up a scandal? Or just to beat the Russians in the Space Race?

Whatever the truth, this viewer has been left with some **unanswered** questions . . .

NOW TRY THESE QUESTIONS . . .

1 Choose the best description for the main message in this article.
   a The Americans were desperate to win the space race.
   b NASA sent cats into space and not men.
   c Men did not really land on the moon – it was faked.

2 What do you think the article wishes to persuade the reader to believe?
   a NASA has always told lies about the moon landing.
   b The Van Allen Belt can cause radiation poisoning.
   c Flags can wave in the wind on the moon.

3 Which of these pieces of information from the article is a clear fact?
   a NASA has been playing a trick on the world.
   b The shadows on the moon photos are in the wrong place.
   c The television show was called 'Conspiracy Theory: Did We Land on the Moon?'

   Now find another fact in the text and write it down as well.

4 Which of these pieces of information from the article is an opinion?
   a On February 15, 2001, the television show was aired in America.
   b The moon landings were set up by NASA on a sound stage in a secret location in the USA and not in space.
   c The programme looked at a lot of NASA photos to prove what it was saying.

   Now find another opinion from the text and write it down as well.

5 What do you think is the writer's opinion about why the Americans might have done something like this? Explain in your own words.

6 Articles can be presented in certain ways to help back up what they are saying. A writer might use different headings, fonts, colours or even pictures to help get their message across.

   How does the picture in this article help to back up the overall message? Choose the most important reason.
   a It makes it more interesting to look at.
   b Colour attracts people to read it.
   c Readers can see things the article is talking about, such as the flag, in the picture.

7 How does the bold print in the article help back up the overall message? Choose the most important reason.
  a The bold words highlight the idea of cheating and the questions being asked.
  b The bold words help to break up the lines and make the article look easier to read.
  c The bold words make the article look more interesting and so more people will read it.

AFTER ANSWERING . . .

Read the notes below to help you think about what you have learned.

The first two questions test whether you have understood the main message and purpose of the text.

Question three shows you that you can do something really important – tell the difference between fact and opinion.

Questions four, five and six look at whether you can spot the difference between facts and opinions in the article.

The last two questions ask you to look at the way the article is presented and if that helps back up what it is saying.

SUMMARY

Remember that:
■ you can prove fact, but opinion is just what someone believes.
Remember to:
■ identify the main purpose
■ identify the ways information is presented
■ look at the colours, fonts and pictures to see the effects of presentation.

WHAT NEXT?

If you need more help with these skills, try quick activities 1 and 2 on page 119. If you think you've got it, you'll have the chance to use them more independently in the Practice section on pages 67–70.

61

PART TWO – FOLLOWING ARGUMENTS AND USING LANGUAGE

YOUR OBJECTIVES ARE . . .

- to show you can follow an argument in a text
- to refer to specific language in the text to help explain your views.

Read this article and then have a go at the questions on pages 63–64.

Review

Conspiracy Theory:
Did We Land on the Moon?

THE PROBLEM with 99 TV channels is having to put up with a lot of dreadful television. Science fiction is a wonderful thing, but it becomes a problem when it is presented as fact.

This brings us to the TV special 'Conspiracy Theory: Did We Land on the Moon?' It's a programme that hopes to convince viewers that NASA faked the Apollo mission moon landings on a movie set.

The TV special gives a long list of supposed 'facts', and with the people interviewed, claims to show that the moon missions were faked. They give all sorts of silly reasons . . . the photography looks wrong, the technology wasn't perfected, the astronauts would have been killed by radiation, the lunar lander was unstable . . . and that's just touching the surface of their mad ideas.

The problem is that, while the TV special does have a certain amount of Jerry Springer-like entertainment value, it displays about as much scientific fact as the average episode of 'Sabrina: The Teenage Witch'.

Any decent scientist can disprove their claims in about two minutes. For example, why is the flag waving? Simple. The astronauts have moved the pole, which moves the flag. You don't need air for this to happen. Why do objects in shadow appear as if they have been lit by a second light source? The objects have been lit by a second light source: the Moon. Light bouncing off the surface of the Moon lights up objects that would otherwise be in complete darkness.

I won't go into any more details here, but it takes you about two minutes of searching on the Internet before you find explanations for the ridiculous claims made in this programme. The makers of it are soon proved to be paranoid idiots.

If you are looking for a laugh or two, this TV special may do the trick. But if you are hoping for any sliver of enlightenment*, you are destined to be disappointed.

*Glossary: sliver of enlightenment = tiny scrap of real information.

NOW TRY THESE QUESTIONS . . .

1 Choose the best description for the main message in this article.
   a The TV programme 'Sabrina: The Teenage Witch' is based on scientific fact.
   b The evidence used in the TV special did not prove what was being said.
   c The TV special was based on facts.

2 What do you think the article wishes to persuade the reader to believe?
   a The Apollo mission moon landings were not faked.
   b Science fiction should be presented as facts.
   c The TV special was a very enlightening programme.

3 Put these statements in the correct order to show what the article does. Think logically. What would you have to do first? What would be sensible to finish with?
   a Summarises its opinion that the programme's claims are wrong.
   b Says the makers of the programme are wrong.
   c Introduces the topic under discussion.
   d Says exactly what is wrong with the claims made by the programme.

4 Which of these quotes is a comparison which shows that the writer thinks the programme is completely wrong?

It displays about as much scientific fact as the average episode of 'Sabrina: The Teenage Witch'.

Any decent scientist can disprove their claims in about two minutes.

They give all sorts of silly reasons.

5 Choose three of these words taken from the article. Put them in a sentence to show that the writer believes the programme to be totally wrong.
- 'ridiculous'   ■ 'idiots'   ■ 'laugh'
- 'dreadful'   ■ 'Jerry Springer-like'   ■ 'simple'

Use the following structure to help you.

The article uses words such as '........' to show you that ....

AFTER ANSWERING . . .

Read the notes below to help you think about what you have learned.

The first two questions test whether you have understood the main message and purpose of the text.

Question three checks you can follow the argument in the article.

The last two questions ask you to show you can use specific words and phrases from the text to back up what you mean.

SUMMARY

Remember to:
- identify the main message
- think about the stages of the argument as a logical sequence
- refer to the language used in the text in your answers.

If you need more help with these skills, try quick activities 1, 2, 5 and 8 on pages 117, 119 and 120. If you think you've got it, you'll have the chance to use them more independently in the Practice section on pages 67–70.

PART THREE – COMPARING TEXTS IN EXAMS

- to compare two different texts
- to identify the similarities and differences between texts.

In Paper One of the GCSE exam it is vital you can compare two different texts and show you recognise how they are similar and how they are different. You are usually told in the question which areas of similarity and difference to look for. Here are some tips for answering this type of question.

- Work on each of the bullet points in the question one by one, in the order that they appear in the question.
- You need to say something about EACH text for each of the bullet points.
- Even if you're not sure about one of the points, never miss it out, or you'll lose a lot of marks.
- Use quotes from both texts wherever you can to back up what you are saying.
- Don't forget you are comparing the two texts, so you must make a comment to show how they are similar or how they are different.
- You may wish to use some of the following phrases in your answer:

  The message in the first text is very different from the second because ....

  The texts are very different here because ....

  The texts are the same when they ....

  The first text uses .... whereas the second chooses to ....

  A good example of this is '..........'

  Although the first text .... , the second ....

  One word which shows this is '..........'

  The article uses words such as '..........' to show you that ....

  To summarise, I would say that ....

NOW TRY THIS QUESTION . . .

Re-read the two articles, 'Did We Really Land on the Moon?' on page 59 and 'Conspiracy Theory: Did We Land On The Moon?' on page 62. Using your answers from Parts One and Two on pages 60–61 and 63–64 , try this exam question.

 Compare the article, 'Did We Really Land on the Moon?' with the review article 'Conspiracy Theory: Did We Land On The Moon?' You should consider the following areas in your answer.

■ The overall message of each.
■ The use of fact and opinion.
■ The use of presentation.
■ The use of language.

AFTER ANSWERING . . .

After you have answered the exam-level question above, work carefully through your writing and check that you have followed the tips for answering. If you find you have missed something, try to improve your answer. If you have followed the advice and used some of the sample phrases, you should feel confident in your skills to compare texts and identify the similarities and differences.

SUMMARY

Remember to:
■ always talk about both texts
■ compare one feature in both texts, then move to the next feature
■ use quotes from both texts, in sentences
■ comment on similarities and differences.

WHAT NEXT?

If you need more help with these skills, try quick activities 1, 2, 5 and 8 on pages 117, 119 and 120. If you think you've got it, you'll have the chance to use them more independently in the Practice section on pages 67–70.

PRACTICE – COMBINING YOUR SKILLS

REMEMBER: the key is to decide what's fact and what's opinion, follow the argument, and recognise the effects of how information is presented.

Read the two texts on this page and on page 68. They are both taken from magazines intended for teenagers and are discussing two sides of the same topic.

A Bad Influence

What's the worst influence on teenage girls in the media?

Internet porn? The club drug scene? GANGSTA RAP CULTURE?

NOTHING so controversial as these. The worst thing teenage girls can do is read **fashion and beauty magazines**.

Have you ever really thought about the images of women and girls in these magazines? Take a look. Do you see anyone over a size 10? Do you see one single spot? Do you see anyone having a bad hair day?

OF COURSE NOT! – But why?

Teen magazines need to sell products, clothes, and images, and pictures of normal, maybe overweight, maybe a bit spotty,

EVERYDAY girls aren't as likely to do it. But because of this, the pictures in teenage magazines convince young girls that unless they are thin, beautiful and expensively dressed, they don't fit in society, aren't as good as everybody else, and need to change! Teenage girls are encouraged by this to go on crazy weight-loss diets and become obsessed with their looks and clothes.

There has recently been an increase in the numbers of young girls who develop eating disorders, because they think

they look fat. Some of these girls are as young as 10! Another worrying trend is the increase in bullying because the victim doesn't wear the 'right' designer labels. The main source of these girls' ideas about their appearance has been teen magazines.

These magazines are the biggest danger to the health and well-being of teenage girls, and should be forced to change before any more damage is done.

■

The Best Friend You Never Knew You Had

There was a girl at our school called Stacey – Stacey Perkins. 'Saddo Stacey' she used to get, right from Year 5 until about the middle of Year 10, when she made the best friend she'd ever had.

You see, Stacey had one of those really old-fashioned mums, who wouldn't let her near make-up, wouldn't let her go out on a weekend on her own, and still chose all her clothes for her. They didn't even have a TV – didn't believe in them. Poor girl. Stacey had no chance really – she was a nice girl, but looked terrible, didn't know anything about music, boys or sport, and liked all the same hobbies as my Gran.

But then, after Christmas in Year 10, Stacey changed.

Suddenly, she started joining in conversations about the R & B charts. She gave Charlotte some really good advice about a little man trouble she'd been having. But most amazing of all, she started to look well . . . cool! It wasn't a massive change – something about the way she brushed her hair and added a little bit of lip gloss, but . . . Stacey was no saddo any more. In fact, Stacey was suddenly an all round necessary person to have in the group, full of chat, info, and mainly . . . confidence!

I asked her one day what had happened to change her, and the answer was amazing. Stacey had an auntie, who had given her a great Christmas present – a subscription to one of the teen magazines for girls.

'Suddenly, I knew what make-up and fashion were all about!' she told me. 'The radio started making sense to me, and those Problem Pages – a mine of information. It's like having a really great friend who'll tell you anything!' Stacey's mum was so pleased with her new-found confidence, she started giving her a bit more freedom – and the rest was history.

'Those magazines saved my life!' said Stacey. And you know what? I went and ordered the same friend for me!

NOW PRACTISE . . .

Getting started

The first question tests whether you have understood the main message and purpose of each article.

1 Explain the main message, or what each article is trying to persuade the reader to believe.

The next step . . .

The next four questions look at whether you can spot the difference between facts and opinions in the articles.

2 The first article, 'A Bad Influence', says that teen magazines are the worst thing that can happen to a teenage girl. Is that a fact or an opinion? Explain your answer.

3 Explain WHY the first article presents the idea that teen magazines are the worst things for teenage girls as a fact. For example,

> *The first article makes the idea that magazines are terrible for teenage girls seem like a fact because it makes the reader* ....

4 The second article, 'The Best Friend You Never Knew You Had', tells the story of how one girl's life was changed in a good way by teen magazines. Could this be a fact? Explain your views and use quotes to support your answer.

5 Explain HOW the second article presents the idea that teen magazines are positive things for teenage girls as a fact. For example,

> *The second article makes the idea that magazines are good for teenage girls seem like a fact because it makes the reader* ....

Thinking about presentation . . .

These two questions ask you to look at the way each article is presented and if that helps back up what it is saying.

6 How does the use of different fonts in the first article help to back up the overall message?

7 What could have been done to the presentation of either article to help back up the message?

Looking at argument . . .

The next question checks that you can follow the argument in each article.

8 Sum up what each of the articles do to put their arguments together. Think logically. What does each article do first? What do they each finish up with? You might want to use some of the statements at the top of page 70.

- Summarises its opinion that the magazines are good/bad.
- Compares magazines to something else to make them seem worse/better.
- Says the magazines are good/bad.
- Introduces the topic under discussion.
- Starts to give details about exactly what is wrong/right with the magazines.
- Gives a final comment about their opinion.

The final step . . .

The last question asks you to show you can use specific words and phrases from the articles to back up what you mean.

9 Select four words or phrases from each text that you think help to summarise what the message is. For example, for the first text you could choose 'damage' and for the second, you might choose 'best friend'.

NOW TRY THIS QUESTION . . .

Using the work you have already done on these articles, try this exam-level question.

Q Compare the articles, 'A Bad Influence' and 'The Best Friend You Never Knew You Had'. You should consider the following areas in your answer.

- **The overall message of each.**
- **The use of fact and opinion.**
- **The use of presentation.**
- **How arguments are structured.**
- **The use of language.**

AFTER ANSWERING . . .

If you have completed all these questions, you can begin to feel confident about your skills with these objectives. Now you are ready to tackle an exam question.

Skill	I need more practice	I usually get it right	I am ready to move on
Tell the difference between fact and opinion			
Understand non-fiction texts			
Recognise the effects of the way information is presented			

PART ONE – ARGUMENT TEXTS

YOUR OBJECTIVES ARE . . .

- to identify the audience and the purpose
- to show you understand how the text is organised
- to comment on the use of language features.

Argument texts are sometimes called discursive texts and they look at two or more sides of an opinion before coming to a decision. They can be written on any topic, but are usually on something that people tend to disagree about.

You may have come across argument texts in newspapers, magazines, leaflets, or even in school, and they are usually quite easy to recognise.

Argument texts usually follow a similar formula.

1 They introduce the topic for discussion.
2 They explain one side of the argument.
3 They explain the opposite side of the argument.
4 They finish off by saying which side they think is right and why.

Argument texts also usually include some specific language features.

- The title, often a question, introduces the topic.
- Rhetorical questions are asked just to make you think about the topic under discussion.
- The text often starts with third person narrative, such as 'He', 'She', 'They', or 'Some people'.
- The text often concludes with first person narrative, such as 'I think' or 'In my opinion'.
- Lots of connectives to help link the ideas and sentences. For example 'however', 'despite this', or 'as well as this.'

Although there can be more to it, most argument texts tend to follow these basic rules.

Now see if you can understand the argument text on page 72. Does it follow the basic rules?

Are TV Pop Competitions the End of Real Music?

In the past few years, television has been jam-packed with programmes running competitions for winners to become rich and famous pop-stars. Shows like 'Pop Idol', 'Fame Academy', and 'PopStars: The Rivals' all keep us glued to the TV to see who will get knocked out, who will win, and who will cry. But are these shows killing real music?

Fans of these types of shows talk about the wonderful opportunities that are offered to people who otherwise might not have had the chance to follow their dreams and become a star. In 2002 Gareth Gates overcame a bad stutter after coming second in the Pop Idol competition and went on to sell millions of CDs. He should have a great future. In the same year 'Fame Academy' gave its winner a million pound recording deal, a swanky flat in London, a sports car and the life of a star for a year. Before winning that competition, David Sneddon had spent months busking in Glasgow, on the dole and going nowhere. You can be sure he doesn't think there is anything wrong with instant fame. And after all, what's wrong with making great television entertainment at the same time as putting a band together?

Despite all this, many people worry that these shows will kill real music. People who work their way through the music industry, who battle to get their demo tapes heard, who face rejection again and again before ever getting close to succeeding, say that just singing a few times on TV isn't the way to build up a music career. They also say that just being able to sing a bit isn't enough – the music industry needs truly talented people who can write their own music and write lyrics that really mean something. Just winning a big karaoke competition on TV, then singing someone else's songs to get a few number one hits does not make for a real star. The instant stars of PopStars will become nobodies again within weeks – just look at Hearsay!

What conclusion can be drawn from all this? Well, as far as I can tell, there are still 40 spots on the chart and those are filled up by whoever the record-buying public like. If these instant stars are so bad, then no-one will buy them for long, and the way will be clear for all these 'real' musicians who, apparently, deserve more of a chance than anyone else. Sounds to me like all the 'real' musicians who haven't made it big are just jealous – or maybe they just aren't good enough! I'm looking forward to the next series of Pop Idol! ■

NOW TRY THESE QUESTIONS . . .

1 Choose the best description of the writer's own opinion.
  a That the competitions are ruining real music.
  b That he could not care less one way or the other.
  c That people should stop moaning about these competitions – they're great.

2 Where does the writer FIRST introduce the topic for discussion?
  a In the first paragraph.
  b Somewhere in the middle.
  c In the title.

3 What is the main reason the writer has used four paragraphs?
  a To make it look better.
  b To impress the examiners.
  c To separate the four parts of the argument.

4 Put in order what the writer does to structure the argument.
  a Summarises with his own opinion about the competition.
  b Explains why some people think the competitions are wrong.
  c Introduces the topic of pop competitions.
  d Explain why some people think the competitions are good.

5 Decide which of these rhetorical questions is most successful in making you think about the issues in the article.
  a 'But are these shows killing real music?'
  b 'What's wrong with great television entertainment at the same time as putting a band together?'
  c 'What conclusion can be drawn from all this?'

6 In which line does the article switch from third to first person narration. Look for the first use of the word 'I'.

7 Find one example of a connecting phrase that the writer uses to link ideas together.

8 Does this text follow the usual rules for argument texts listed on page 71? Give three examples to back up your answer.

AFTER ANSWERING . . .

You should now have a good idea of how argument texts are organised and what language features they tend to use. You should be able to recognise an argument text if one comes up in the exam.

SUMMARY

Remember to:
- identify the purpose and the writer's opinion
- look at how the text is organised to present the argument
- look for the language features used in an argument
- refer to the text in your answers.

WHAT NEXT?

If you need more help with these skills, try quick activities 1, 2, 5–8 and 10 on pages 117, 119–120 and 122. If you think you've got it, you'll have the chance to write your own argument texts in the Practice section on pages 81–83.

PART TWO – PERSUASIVE TEXTS

YOUR OBJECTIVES ARE . . .
- to identify the audience and the purpose
- to show you understand how the text is organised
- to comment on the use of language and presentation features.

Persuasive texts also argue a case for a particular point of view, but mainly try to convince you to think or do something. They can be written on any topic and can be quite sneaky in the ways that they try to persuade you.

You may have come across persuasive texts in newspapers, magazines, or leaflets, on TV, or even on the Internet, and they are not always easy to recognise. Advertisements are persuasive texts, but do you always realise when a text is trying to sell you an idea or a product?

Persuasive texts can follow a similar formula to argument texts.

1 They introduce the topic for discussion.
2 They explain their opinion, giving key points to back up what they believe.
3 They explain why they think the opposite opinion is wrong.
4 They finish off by repeating why their opinion is the right one.

However, persuasive texts can be organised in many ways, so you have to be on your toes, thinking about what the PURPOSE of any text might be. If it's trying to convince you to think or do something, it's a persuasive text.

Persuasive texts also usually include some specific language and presentation features.

- The title, often a question, introduces the topic.
- Rhetorical questions are asked just to make you think about the topic under discussion.
- First (e.g. 'I'), second (e.g. 'you'), or third (e.g. 'he' or 'they') person narrative depending on the effect they want.
- Pictures, colour and different fonts to help back up the point of view.

- Lots of EMOTIVE language that makes people feel strong emotions.
- Lots of tricks, like rhythm or alliteration, to make words and phrases sound better.
- Short punchy sentences to create impact.
- Lots of connectives to help link the ideas and sentences. For example 'because', 'therefore', or 'as well as this.'

Although there can be more to it, most persuasive texts tend to follow these basic rules.

Now see if you can understand this persuasive advert from AXA Sunlife. Does it follow the basic rules?

'For A Richer Future Start Saving Today' says Leslie Ash

And after 12 months you'll get half your money back

'A new home, the car you've always dreamt of, the holiday of a lifetime . . . We all have a dream. And now there's a way to help make your dreams come true. It's a special plan where you start saving today ready for tomorrow, *without* being strapped for cash. Just put a bit away each month with the Bonus Cashbuilder Plus plan, and your money can quickly add up. So why not start saving from just £10 a month today?' says Leslie Ash.

Imagine not having to worry about money, and being able to treat yourself to **life's little luxuries**. Driving around in **the car of your dreams** or jetting off on the **exotic holiday** you never thought you'd be able to afford.

There IS a way to help you afford any of these things or simply build a nest-egg for the future. With the **Bonus CashBuilder Plus** savings plan, it's up to you how much you invest. You can start saving from just £10 a month or you can pay more, up to £100 a month.

Remarkably, after saving for just 12 months you will receive cashback equal to HALF your premiums paid.

As Bonus CashBuilder Plus is a unique 15 year savings scheme, in the year 2018 you could receive a cheque for thousands of pounds, to spend as you like.

And just for enquiring about the plan you will be sent a **FREE Parker pen**.

This *special cashback opportunity* cannot be repeated. So, if you are interested, don't delay. Find out more today. Just call our FREEPHONE number or fill out and send the coupon opposite to the FREEPOST address on it.

'Your dreams could come true when your Bonus CashBuilder Plus matures.'

NOW TRY THESE QUESTIONS . . .

1 Choose the best description of the purpose of this text.
  a To persuade you to buy a new car.
  b To persuade you to start saving money with this plan.
  c To persuade you to like Leslie Ash.

2 When does the writer FIRST introduce the thing it is trying to persuade you to do?
  a In the first paragraph.
  b In the title.
  c Somewhere in the middle.

3 Put into order exactly what the writer does to structure the text.
  a Summarises with a positive statement about the plan.
  b Gives you a good reason to find out more about it all.
  c Introduces the topic of saving money for the future.
  d Gives a positive celebrity opinion of the savings plan.
  e Explains why the savings plan is a good thing, using various key points.

4 Which of the following does this persuasive text NOT do? Think about WHY.
  a Include any bad points about giving this company your money.
  b Offer you a free gift for finding out more.
  c Suggest ways you could spend the money.

5 How do the pictures with this text help to back up what it is trying to do?

6 Look at all the words that are made to stand out in capitals, bold or italics. They are all emotive words, which create an emotional reaction in people. They also give a very positive impression of this plan. Try to complete the following sentences with some more detail about this.

   a The advert puts 'the car of your dreams' and 'exotic holiday' in bold because these phrases make the reader think of ....
   b The words 'special cashback opportunity' are in italics to make the reader think that this savings plan is ....
   c The advert says in bold italics that 'dreams could come true' because it wants the reader to ....
   d The advert puts the words 'freepost' and 'freephone' in capitals because it wants to encourage the reader to ....

7 Does this text follow any of the usual rules for persuasion texts explained on page 74? Give three examples to help back up your answer.

AFTER ANSWERING . . .

You should now have a good idea of how persuasive texts are organised and what language features and presentation tricks they tend to use. You should be able to recognise a persuasive text if one comes up in the exam.

SUMMARY

Remember to:
- identify the purpose of the text
- identify the writer's opinion
- look at how the text is organised to persuade
- look for the language and presentation features used to persuade
- refer to the text in your answers.

WHAT NEXT?

If you need more help with these skills, try quick activities 1, 2, 5–8 and 10 on pages 117, 119–120 and 122. If you think you've got it, you'll have the chance to write your own persuasive text in the Practice section on pages 84–86.

PART THREE – ADVICE TEXTS

YOUR OBJECTIVES ARE . . .

- to identify the audience and the purpose
- to show you understand how the text is organised
- to comment on the use of language and presentation features.

Advice texts give you guidance or recommendations to help you to do something or to decide about something. Remember, advice is more than a list of instructions.

You will have used advice texts, maybe without even realising it. If you've ever taken notice of a poster at the dentist's on why and how you should clean your teeth or followed the tips in a fishing magazine on how to catch the best fish, you've used an advice text. You may have come across advice texts in newspapers, magazines, leaflets, or even in school, and they are usually quite easy to recognise.

Advice texts usually follow the same formula.

1 They introduce the topic for advice, often with a question.
2 They are written in chronological, or time, order.
3 They go through key points that you must consider, often in the form of commands.
4 They might include diagrams to give further advice (although you will not be given any marks for including a diagram in an exam answer).
5 They may finish off with a checklist of what should be done.

Advice texts also usually include some specific language features.

- The title, often a question, introduces the topic.
- Second person narrative to talk directly to the reader, such as 'You …….. should ……..' or 'Then you should ……..'.
- Encouraging words to make what you have to do seem easy, so you feel confident.
- Lots of time connectives to help link the ideas and sentences, such as 'First of all', 'Next', or 'Finally.'
- Straightforward language to make it easy to follow, except if they have to use specialist words for equipment.

Although there can be more to it, advice texts tend to follow many of these basic rules.

Can you understand this advice text? Does it follow the basic rules?

safecomputing

You might be surprised to learn that your computer could do permanent damage to your body! However, after just a few months spent hunched over a keyboard, it is surprising just how many aches and pains you can develop. Some people also get a condition called repetitive strain injury or RSI, which makes their hands, wrists and arms very painful. RSI is caused by making the same small movements over and over again, and by sitting slumped in a chair. So create an environment for safe computing!

Organising your desk

The first thing you need to do is organise your desk properly. Use one that is large enough for the computer, monitor, and keyboard. If the monitor is separate, it is best to put the computer under the desk to leave more space for you to work on top. You will also need to think about where to put any other hardware you might have, such as a printer and a scanner.

It is worth looking at the space on the desk top. Is there enough space for any reference papers you need and to move the mouse around easily?

Before you think the desk's perfect, make sure it doesn't wobble. If it does, wedge something underneath the wobbly leg.

Sitting comfortably

Next pay attention to the type of chair you use. An office-style chair is best so you can alter the height and adjust the back to the correct angle. If you can't get one of these chairs, you can improvise. Your feet should rest comfortably on the floor – if they don't, rest them on something solid like a box. Your lower back should be straight and supported – if it's not, use a cushion and think 'straight!'.

Last, but definitely not least, make sure that when you are keying, your wrists are in line with the floor – if they're not, you need to sit on a cushion or raise the keyboard.

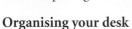

NOW TRY THESE QUESTIONS . . .

1 Choose the best description of the purpose of this text.
 a To persuade you to make better use of your PC.
 b To advise you on how to use your computer without damaging your body.
 c To advise you on how to choose the best office-style chair.

2 Where does the writer FIRST introduce the things he is trying to advise you about?
 a In the first paragraph.
 b In the title.
 c Somewhere in the middle.

3 Put into order exactly what the writer does to structure the advice.

  a Divides the text with headings and into paragraphs.

  b Introduces the idea of damaging your body.

  c Goes through key things that you must do, usually in the form of commands.

  d Discusses the reasons why you should take the advice.

4 Does the picture with this text help to back up what it is trying to do? If so, how?

5 Sort the following words into four types using a grid like the one below the words.

  ■ organise   ■ keying   ■ before   ■ make sure
  ■ RSI   ■ last   ■ use   ■ it is worth
  ■ you need   ■ create   ■ monitor   ■ next
  ■ hardware   ■ adjust   ■ first   ■ is best

Specialist words	Words for WHEN to do something (Time connectives)	Words for WHAT to do (Imperative verbs)	Advice words

6 Does this text follow any of the usual rules for advice texts explained on page 78? Give three examples to help back up your answer.

AFTER ANSWERING . . .

You should have a good idea of how advice texts are organised and what language features and presentation tricks they tend to use. You should be able to recognise an advice text if one comes up in the exam.

SUMMARY

Remember to:

■ identify the purpose of the text

■ look at how the text is organised to advise

■ look for the language and presentation features used to advise

■ refer to the text in your answers.

WHAT NEXT?

If you need more help with these skills, try quick activities 1, 2, 5–8 and 10 on pages 117, 119–120 and 122. If you think you've got it, you'll have the chance to write your own advice texts in the Practice section on pages 87–88.

PRACTICE – WRITING ARGUMENT TEXTS

REMEMBER: the key to writing your own argument text is to think about your reader and purpose, organise your writing, and choose appropriate language.

Need to remind yourself of the basic rules for writing an argument text? If you do, look back at page 71.

NOW PRACTISE . . .

Getting started

1 Write an argument text which considers the following question.

Should the system of film classification by age be abolished?

The first step is to think of some reasons for and against getting rid of film classification. Use a chart like the one below to help you. Some ideas have already been filled in to give you a start.

Film classification should be abolished	Film classification should be kept
We should be allowed to decide for ourselves.	Seeing some films could increase children's nightmares.
It should be up to parents to decide for their own child.	Some films might be a bad influence, encouraging people to extremes of violence.
Rules are already broken, especially with videos, so why bother with them?	Some films could increase children's use of bad language.

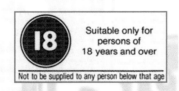

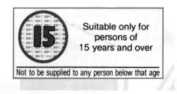

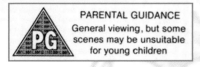

Now start to write . . .

2 Remember the question that you are answering is about film classification. It's up to you if you think it should be abolished or not.

Follow the plan below to help you. It shows you the structure that argument texts should follow in four parts. You could use four paragraphs in your writing, one for each section.

PARAGRAPH ONE

Introduce the topic by saying what film classification is. For example,

Film classification is a system used in Britain which decides who can watch films at the cinema, according to how old they are. For example, ...

PARAGRAPH TWO

Explain one side of the argument and give some detailed reasons to support it. For example,

Many people believe that film classification is against our human rights and that ....

PARAGRAPH THREE

Explain the opposite side of the argument and give some detailed reasons to support it. For example,

Despite this, other people believe that ....

PARAGRAPH FOUR

Conclude by saying which side you think is right and – most importantly – why. For example,

In my opinion, film classification is ....

Keep referring back to the language rules explained on page 71 as you write. Are you including rhetorical questions? Starting with third person narrative? Concluding with first person narrative? Using a lot of connectives?

Use the following connective words to help you complete your writing.

- For example
- As a result of this
- Some might say
- Because of this
- This view is supported by the fact that
- Alternatively
- As evidence of this
- In conclusion
- Clearly
- It is clear that
- We can see that
- Therefore

More practice . . .

3 The examiners could ask you to write an argument text on any topic. Have a go at this exam-level question to perfect your technique.

 You are a member of the Sports Council. The Council is considering whether gyms and swimming pools should be free as part of the National Health Service. Write a speech to be presented to the Council in which you ARGUE both FOR and AGAINST this idea.

AFTER ANSWERING . . .

If you have completed all these questions, you can begin to feel confident about your skills with these objectives. Look at the checklist below and grade your skills to make sure you're ready to tackle an exam question.

Skill	I need more practice	I usually get it right	I am ready to move on
Identify my reader and purpose			
Structure my argument			
Organise sentences well			
Use paragraphs effectively			
Use punctuation accurately			
Use appropriate words for argument			
Spell words correctly			

WHAT NEXT?

If you need more help with writing non-fiction texts, try quick activities 2 and 11 on pages 123 and 128.

PRACTICE – WRITING PERSUASIVE TEXTS

 REMEMBER: the key to writing your own persuasive text is to think about your reader and purpose, organise your writing, and choose appropriate language.

If you need to remind yourself of the basic rules for writing a persuasive text, look back at page 74.

NOW PRACTISE . . .

Getting started

In the past, examiners have asked students to write one of many types of persuasive texts, from leaflets about health to letters to friends who are thinking of running away.

1 Write a text which persuades people to become a member of their local gym. The first step is to think of some good reasons for joining a gym. Next plan which of the language and presentation tricks you'll use in your text to help persuade people this is a good idea.

Use a chart like the one below to help you. Some ideas have already been filled in to give you a start.

Good reasons for joining a gym

Improve stamina levels.

Improve looks.

Meet new people.

Language and presentation tricks to use

Using rhetorical questions, such as 'Do you look as good as you could?'

Use a lot of emotive language, such as 'Stop being fat and lazy: become fit and sexy.'

Use bold to make key words stand out.

Now start to write . . .

2 Remember your purpose is to try to persuade people to join a gym, so don't say anything negative about it.

Follow the plan below to help you. It shows you the structure that argument texts should follow in four parts. You could use four paragraphs in your writing, one for each section.

PARAGRAPH ONE

Introduce the topic by starting to talk about why anyone should join a gym. For example,

Now Christmas is over, are you left with too many pounds around the waist? We can provide the solution to ....

PARAGRAPH TWO

Explain one opinion, giving key points to back up what you believe. For example,

There are many benefits to joining a gym and attending regularly. Your general health and well being ....

PARAGRAPH THREE

Explain why you think the opposite opinion is wrong. For example,

If you are committed to fitness, there is no reason why you should not make a huge difference ....

PARAGRAPH FOUR

Finish off by repeating why your opinion is the right one and make a final persuasive statement. For example,

If you want to improve your life, joining a gym is the best step you can ....

Use the following connective words to help you complete your writing.

- For example
- Also
- Consequently
- Clearly
- This view is supported by the fact that
- The effect of this
- We can see that
- In conclusion
- Some people imagine that
- As evidence of this
- In addition to this
- Because of this

More practice . . .

3 The examiners could ask you to write a persuasive text on any topic. Have a go at this exam-level question to perfect your technique.

 Imagine your Headteacher has decided the school will have a fund raising event for a charity chosen by the students. Choose the charity you think is most deserving and write a document to give to all students to PERSUADE them to vote for your charity.

AFTER ANSWERING . . .

If you have completed all these questions, you can begin to feel confident about your skills with these objectives. Look at the checklist below and grade your skills to make sure you're ready to tackle an exam question.

Skill	I need more practice	I usually get it right	I am ready to move on
Identify my reader and purpose			
Structure my argument			
Organise sentences well			
Use paragraphs effectively			
Use punctuation accurately			
Use appropriate words for argument			
Spell words correctly			

WHAT NEXT?

If you need more help with writing non-fiction texts, try quick activities 2 and 11 on pages 123 and 128.

PRACTICE – WRITING ADVICE TEXTS

REMEMBER: the key to writing your own advice text is to think about your reader and purpose, organise your writing and choose appropriate language.

If you need to remind yourself of the basic rules for writing an advice text, look back at page 78.

NOW PRACTISE . . .

Getting started

1 Write a text which advises people on how to plan a day trip on a bike.

The first step is to think of exactly what each stage in the planning should be – if you miss anything out, the cyclists could end up being stranded! Think about what tips for success you can give, rather than just writing a list of instructions. You can't assume anything about what people already know. Next plan the language you'll use in your text to make sure your advice is clear.

Use a chart like the one below to help you. Some ideas have already been filled in to give you a start.

Equipment needed

Puncture repair kit.

Map of the area.

Steps in planning or advice

Make sure you are fit enough before you plan to cycle for a full day.

Tell someone where you are going.

Specialist language that may need explanation

Panniers.

Puncture.

Waterproofs.

2 Before you start to write this up, test out your plan for the text on a class mate. They might notice you have forgotten to suggest taking lunch.

Use the following connective words to help you complete your writing.

- First of all
- Next
- Finally
- In the end

- After that
- Then
- Take the
- Check that

- If you find that
- Make sure that
- Do not forget to
- When this is completed

More practice . . .

3 The examiners could ask you to write an advice text on any topic. Have a go at this exam-level question.

Q **You are a local doctor. You have decided to write a short leaflet to ADVISE teenagers on simple ways they can eat a healthy diet and get enough exercise. Write the text for the leaflet.**

AFTER ANSWERING . . .

If you have completed all these questions, you can begin to feel confident. Look at the checklist below and grade your skills to make sure you're ready to tackle an exam question.

Skill	I need more practice	I usually get it right	I am ready to move on
Identify my reader and purpose			
Structure my advice			
Organise sentences well			
Use paragraphs effectively			
Use punctuation accurately			
Use appropriate words to advise			
Spell words correctly			

WHAT NEXT?

If you need more help with writing non-fiction texts, try quick activities 2 and 11 on pages 123 and 128.

PART ONE — INFORMATION TEXTS

YOUR OBJECTIVES ARE . . .

- to identify the audience and the purpose
- to show you understand how the text is organised
- to comment on the use of language features.

Information texts are written to give the reader information about a topic. They can be written on absolutely any topic, from simple examples like a train timetable to an essay on nuclear physics.

You will have come across information texts everywhere — in the street, newspapers, magazines, leaflets, or even in school, and they are usually quite easy to recognise.

Information texts usually follow the same formula.

1 They introduce the topic for discussion, sometimes just with a title.
2 They begin to give information about the general topic.
3 They may then split the information up into categories to make it easier to follow.
4 They may include tables, diagrams or illustrations to add further information.

Information texts also usually include some specific language and presentation features.

- Third person narrative is usual, such as 'This is' or 'Some people'.
- Specific examples may be included to give more information.
- Straightforward language to make it easy to follow, except if they have to use specialist words for technical terms or equipment.
- Lots of connectives to help link the ideas and sentences, such as 'then', 'because' or 'so that.'

Although there can be more to it than this, most information texts tend to follow these basic rules.

Now see if you can understand the information text on page 90. Does it follow the basic rules?

skateboarding science

Skateboards – some people think they are just planks of wood with wheels, others know they are highly engineered devices which have been honed* and developed extensively over the years.

The basic elements which make up a skateboard are the board (deck), the wheels and the trucks – the part which connects the wheels to the deck and allows it to turn. Modern skateboard decks can be made from modern materials, but many professionals still find sugar maple wood is better.

The shape of the board is individual to each rider – the way the board curves up at the edges, nose, and tail strengthens the board and gives the rider more control. The board shape has evolved as riding styles have changed.

Skateboard wheels play a major part in the riding experience. Early wheels were made of steel and offered little traction, which limited the number of tricks which could be done. In the 1970s urethane wheels were created which made the whole ride smoother and easier to control.

Steering a skateboard is down to the trucks which are attached to the underside of the board, and to the wheels, via an axle which allows the wheel to swing. By leaning to the left or right on a board you can change the direction of travel.

Skateboard design is more about getting it right for the rider than having the best-looking board with the latest design. You can have a board which is technically perfect and where the engineering and the physics are second to none – but if it does not feel right to the rider they will not ride it!

*Glossary: honed = improved.
Article from www.noisenet.ws

NOW TRY THESE QUESTIONS . . .

1 Where does the writer FIRST introduce the topic?
a In the first paragraph.
b Somewhere in the middle.
c In the title.

2 What is the main reason the writer has split the text into six paragraphs?
  a To make it look better.
  b To separate the different sections of information.
  c To impress the examiners.

3 The writer structures the information very carefully. Put these statements in the correct order.
  a Gives information about the wheels.
  b Rounds off by saying how important careful design is.
  c Gives information about the trucks.
  d Introduces the idea of skateboards being carefully designed.
  e Gives information about the shape.
  f Gives information about what makes up a skateboard.

4 Which of these words are specialist words for technical terms or equipment?
  ■ design   ■ trucks   ■ shape
  ■ axle   ■ urethane   ■ traction

5 How could the writer have made it easier to understand what some of the specialist words mean?

6 Does this text follow the usual rules for information texts explained on page 89? Give three examples to help back up your answer.

AFTER ANSWERING . . .

You should now have a good idea of how information texts are organised and what language features they tend to use. You should be able to recognise an information text if one comes up in the exam.

SUMMARY

Remember to:
- identify the purpose of the text
- look at how the text is organised to give information
- look for the language features used to inform
- refer to the text in your answers.

WHAT NEXT?

If you need more help with these skills, try quick activities 1, 2, 5–8 and 10 on pages 117, 119–120 and 122. If you think you've got it, you'll have the chance to use write your own information texts in the Practice section on pages 98–100.

PART TWO – EXPLANATION TEXTS

YOUR OBJECTIVES ARE . . .

- to identify the audience and the purpose
- to show you understand how the text is organised
- to comment on the use of language and presentation features.

Explanation texts give you information and reasons to help you understand how and why something is as it is. They may be on how something works or on why someone feels the way they do. They can be written on any topic, from simple signs to explain why something is closed, to an essay on world history.

You will have come across information texts everywhere – in the street, newspapers, magazines, leaflets, or even in school, and they are usually quite easy to recognise.

Explanation texts can follow a similar formula to informative texts, although there are some differences too.

1 They introduce the topic for discussion, sometimes just with a title or question.
2 They begin to explain the general topic.
3 They may split the general topic into categories to make it easier to follow.
4 They may order the explanation step by step to make it easier to follow.
5 They may include tables, checklists or illustrations (although you will not be given marks for including these in an exam answer).
6 They may conclude with a summary.

Explanation texts also usually include some specific language and presentation features.

- The question to be answered is often used to begin. This may start with 'How?' or 'Why?'.
- Third person narrative is usual, such as 'This is' or 'Some people'.
- Attractive layout to make it appealing to read.
- Specific examples may be included to give more information.
- Straightforward language to make it easy to follow, except if they have to use specialist words for technical terms or equipment.
- Lots of connectives to help link the ideas and sentences, such as 'then', 'because', 'gradually', or 'so that.'

Now see if you can understand the following explanation text. Does it follow any of the basic rules?

Why do we dream?

A lot of people have some interesting ideas about dreams. There are physiological, psychological and spiritual explanations.

'Physiological' has to do with how the body works. Some scientists think maybe we dream in order to exercise our brains. When you are awake, messages are constantly speeding among all your billions of brain cells to keep you moving, thinking, digesting, and so on. So the idea is that when you are asleep, dreams exercise the 'pathways' between the brain cells.

Then there's the 'psychological' set of ideas about why we dream. Psychology has to do with your thoughts and emotions. Most dreams are actually about immediate concerns in our lives. Some dreams may help us know more about ourselves. Others might be practice for dealing with daytime problems. Dreams can be about fears, wishes, plans, hopes, and worries. The famous Sigmund Freud, who gave us a lot of ideas about how our minds work, was very interested in interpreting dreams. He thought that dreams contained symbols of things hidden deep within our minds and memories.

A lot of people think dreams must be more complicated than this. They could have a spiritual explanation, connected to our inner selves or to religious things. In lots of religions and cultures, dreams are thought to be prophetic, meaning they can predict the future. Some people believe they can contact the dead through their dreams, and even travel to places and see the world.

Despite all these theories, it is still not possible to prove that just one of these theories is correct. Perhaps it is a combination of all three!

NOW TRY THESE QUESTIONS . . .

1 Choose the best description of the purpose of this text.
   a To say that dreams are caused by day time fears.
   b To explain the different theories about dreams.
   c To talk about different types of dreams.

2 Where does the writer FIRST introduce the thing he is trying to explain to you?
   a In the first paragraph.
   b In the title.
   c Somewhere in the middle.

3 The writer structures the text very carefully. Put these statements in the correct order.
   a Gives the spiritual theory about dreams.
   b Begins to explain the different theories about dreams.
   c Gives the psychological theory about dreams.
   d Concludes with a summary of the theories.
   e Gives the physiological theory about dreams.
   f Introduces dreams with a question in the title.

4 What other pictures would have backed up the message?

5 Does this text follow the usual rules for explanation texts listed on page 92? Give three examples to back up your answer.

AFTER ANSWERING . . .

You should now have a good idea of how explanation texts are organised and what language features and types of presentation they tend to use. You should be able to recognise an explanation text if one comes up in the exam.

SUMMARY

Remember to:
- identify the purpose of the text
- look at how the text is organised to give explanations
- look for the language and presentation features to explain
- refer to the text in your answers.

WHAT NEXT?

If you need more help with these skills, try quick activities 1, 2, 5–8 and 10 on pages 117, 119–120 and 122. If you think you've got it, you'll have the chance to write your own explanation text in the Practice section on pages 101–103.

PART THREE – DESCRIPTION TEXTS

YOUR OBJECTIVES ARE . . .

- to identify the audience and the purpose
- to show you understand how the text is organised
- to comment on the use of language and presentation features.

Description texts are written to give you details on what something is like.

You may have come across these texts in newspapers, magazines, leaflets, or even in school, and they are usually quite easy to recognise. They might give technical information about something, be part of an autobiography or even part of a holiday brochure. The purpose is to create a picture of what is being described in the reader's mind.

Description texts tend to follow the same formula.

1 They introduce the topic to be described.
2 They may then split the main topic into categories to make it easier to follow.
3 Each section will contain plenty of descriptive detail.
4 They may conclude with a summary.

Description texts also usually include some specific language and presentation features.

- Third person narrative, such as 'This is' or 'Some people', may be used, especially for more technical descriptions.
- First person narrative, such as 'I remember', may be used for an autobiographical description.
- Pictures to make it appealing to read and to add detail.
- Lots of adjectives and adverbs to build up description.
- Similes and metaphors to help add to the description.
- Connectives to link the ideas and sentences, such as 'as well as this', 'similarly,' or 'and.'

Now see if you can understand the description text from *Improve Your Coarse Fishing* magazine on page 96. Does it follow any of the basic rules?

Beautiful Fisheries in Yorkshire

ANY FISHERMAN or woman would be happy to spend a day at Guscott Farm Fishery in West Yorkshire. I spent a wonderful day there recently, happily admiring the sights and sounds of this small but stunning haven for fishermen, professional and amateur alike.

The lake is in a perfect spot, just behind a clump of oak trees and balanced on the brow of a hill. The view is amazing, with miles of fields and villages laid out before you. Time seems to stand still, as you gaze across the waters to tiny tractors and haystacks in the middle distance.

The lake itself is a mine of quiet activity. The cool green waters are lined with reeds and rushes, all buzzing with dragonflies and you can hear the gentle popping of giant carp feeding at the surface. As one of the fisherman, you feel a part of the natural landscape as you quietly sit and wait, hoping for a bite, searching for those giveaway bubbles.

As the sun sets and shadows creep across the lake, your luminous float becomes harder and harder to spot. A small catch – a perfect shining mirror carp, with its small mouth gaping and large scales glistening as you gently release it back into the water. You know it's time to pack up and go home, but that last chance of a big catch makes you want to stay in the cool and peaceful atmosphere.

With only two small mirror carp and a good bream all day, you'd think I wouldn't want to return – but you'd be wrong. I look forward to my next visit to this beautiful, undisturbed, and relaxing place.

NOW TRY THESE QUESTIONS . . .

1 Choose the best description of the MAIN purpose of this text.
  a To persuade you that this place is the very best for fishing.
  b To give you information about the fish to be caught there.
  c To describe the whole place.

2 What other, less important, purposes does this text have?
  a To inform.　　　**b** To advise.
  c To persuade.　　**d** Another purpose.

3 Does the picture with this text back up the purpose? Explain.

4 Sort these words into three types in a chart like the one below.
  ■ amateur　■ tiny　■ float　■ as
  ■ shining　■ with　■ giveaway　■ and
  ■ mirror carp　■ scales　■ green　■ bream
  ■ but　■ perfect　■ undisturbed　■ catch

Specialist words	Descriptive words (Adjectives and adverbs)	Connecting words

5 Does this text follow any of the usual rules for description texts as explained on page 95? Give three examples of how it does.

AFTER ANSWERING . . .

You should now have a good idea of how description texts are organised and what language features and presentation tricks they tend to use. You should be able to recognise a description text if one comes up in the exam.

SUMMARY

Remember to:
■ identify the purpose of the text
■ look at how the text is organised to give descriptions
■ look for the language and presentation features used to describe
■ refer to the text in your answers.

WHAT NEXT?

If you need more help with these skills, try quick activities 1, 2, 5–8 and 10 on page 117, 119–120 and 122. If you think you've got it, you'll have the chance to write your own descriptive texts in the Practice section on pages 104–105.

PRACTICE – WRITING INFORMATION TEXTS

REMEMBER: the key to writing your own information text is to think about your reader and purpose, organise your writing, and choose appropriate language.

Need to remind yourself of the basic rules for writing an information text? If you do, look back at page 89.

NOW PRACTISE . . .

Getting started

1 Write an information text which considers the following topic.

The different types of programme available to watch on British television.

The first step is to think of a list of types of programme, what they include, and some examples of them. Use a chart like the one below to help you. Some ideas have already been filled in to give you a start.

Type of programme	What it includes	Some real examples
Soap	Over the top drama about everyday lives; lots of plot lines about love, sex, crime, and misery.	Eastenders, Coronation Street, Home and Away.
Sport	Live transmission or real sport, commentary, interviews with sport stars, sports awards ceremonies.	Match of the Day, Grandstand, NBA Live.
News		
Cookery		
Cartoons		
Comedy		

Now select three of these types of programmes to write about in your answer. They should be the ones you know most about.

Now start to write . . .

2 Follow the plan below to help you answer the question. It shows you the structure that information texts should follow. It uses an introduction before continuing with separate sections for each type of programme and then has a summary paragraph at the end.

PARAGRAPH ONE

Introduce the topic by saying what types of programme there are and maybe why there are so many in the UK. For example,

In the UK there are many different types of ....

PARAGRAPH TWO

Focus on just one type of programme and include all the information you have planned. For example,

One type of programme which is very popular is ....

PARAGRAPH THREE

Now include all the information you had planned for the next type of programme.

Another type of programme which is screened a lot on British television is ....

PARAGRAPH FOUR

Focus on just another type of programme and include all the information you had planned. For example,

'..........' is another very popular type of programme and ....

PARAGRAPH FIVE

Summarise all your information and perhaps add a final bit of information. For example,

There are so many types of programme available to watch in the UK that ....

Keep referring back to the language rules explained on page 89 as you write.

Use the following connective words to help you complete your writing.

- *As well as this*
- *Similarly*
- *Secondly*
- *Then*
- *And so*
- *Finally*
- *Additionally*
- *Furthermore*
- *Another example of this*

More practice . . .

3 The examiners could ask you to write an information text on any topic. Have a go at this exam-level question to perfect your technique.

 There are many different types of music in the charts. Choose three types that you enjoy and know a lot about. Write about these types of music in a way which will INFORM other people.

AFTER ANSWERING . . . ●●●

If you have completed all these questions, you can begin to feel confident about your skills with these objectives. Look at the checklist below and grade your skills to make sure you're ready to tackle an exam question.

Skill	I need more practice	I usually get it right	I am ready to move on
Identify my reader and purpose			
Structure my information			
Organise sentences well			
Use paragraphs effectively			
Use punctuation accurately			
Use appropriate words to inform			
Spell words correctly			

WHAT NEXT?

If you need more help with writing non-fiction texts, try quick activities 2 and 11 on pages 123 and 128.

PRACTICE – WRITING EXPLANATION TEXTS

REMEMBER: the key to writing your own explanation text is to think about your reader and purpose, organise your writing, and choose appropriate language.

If you need to remind yourself of the basic rules for writing an explanation text, look back at page 92.

NOW PRACTISE . . .

Getting started

1 Write a text which explains why fast food is bad for us.

You may need to complete some research first to help you answer this question. Use a chart like the one below to help you research the topic. Some ideas have already been filled in to give you a start.

Why Fast Food is Bad for Us	
1 Too much fat in most fast foods.	Burgers, chips, pizzas and doughnuts can contain 50% fat, which is bad for the heart.
2 Makes us put on weight.	Extra weight makes us feel unhealthy and act more lazily.
3	
4	

Now start to write . . .

2 Remember your purpose. You are trying to explain to people why fast food is bad for us, so you need to include plenty of extra detail to back up your explanations. Follow this plan to help you.

PARAGRAPH ONE

Introduce the topic by starting to talk about the problem with fast food. For example,

Fast food is becoming ever more popular in this country, but it is not ....

PARAGRAPH TWO

Begin to explain one reason why it is bad for us, giving key points to back up what you are saying. For example,

The amount of saturated fat contained in many fast foods ....

PARAGRAPH THREE

Begin to explain the next reason why it is bad for us, giving key points to back up what you are saying. For example,

Many fast foods ....

PARAGRAPH FOUR

Begin to explain another reason why it is bad for us, giving key points to back up what you are saying. For example,

In addition to this, ...

PARAGRAPH FIVE

Summarise and perhaps add a final bit of information. For example,

The biggest problem with fast food is that ....

Keep referring back to the language rules explained on page 92 as you write.

Use the following connective words to help you complete your writing.

- In conclusion
- We can see that
- Consequently
- Because of this
- This view is supported by the fact that
- The effect of this
- As evidence of this
- In addition to this
- Some people imagine that
- For example
- Also
- Clearly

More practice . . .

3 The examiners could ask you to write an explanation text on any topic. Have a go at this exam-level question to perfect your technique.

 Many people enjoy playing a sport as a hobby. Choose a sport you enjoy or know well. Write an article for a magazine to EXPLAIN the important rules of the sport and how to play it well.

AFTER ANSWERING . . .

If you have completed all these questions, you can begin to feel confident about your skills with these objectives. Look at the checklist below and grade your skills to make sure you're ready to tackle an exam question.

Skill	I need more practice	I usually get it right	I am ready to move on
Identify my reader and purpose			
Structure my explanation			
Organise sentences well			
Use paragraphs effectively			
Use punctuation accurately			
Use appropriate words to explain			
Spell words correctly			

WHAT NEXT?

If you need more help with writing non-fiction texts, try quick activities 2 and 11 on pages 123 and 128.

PRACTICE – WRITING DESCRIPTION TEXTS

PRACTISE SKILLS FROM PART THREE

REMEMBER: the key to writing your own description text is to think about your reader and purpose, organise your writing, and choose appropriate language.

If you need to remind yourself of the basic rules for writing an description text, look back at page 95.

NOW PRACTISE . . .

Getting started

1 Write a text which describes in detail somewhere you have been on holiday, somewhere you know well, or even the place in the photograph.

The first step is to think of your ideas and plan your writing. You need to think of three or four separate sections to build into paragraphs. For example, if you choose to write about a holiday in Cyprus, you might focus on the hotel, beach, town area, and a castle too.

Use a spider diagram like the one below to help you plan the sections AND the detail you are going to include. Some ideas have already been filled in to give you a start.

Feel of hot silky sand. Smell of so much sun tan oil. Fantastic view of water sports and the cliffs.

Hotel

Cyprus

Town

Beach

Castle

2 Now check you have enough ideas on how to write about the descriptive detail. You can use adjectives and adverbs to do this, if you choose the words with care.

Remember, adverbs describe how something is done and often end in 'ly', for example 'it floated softly' or 'he spoke crossly'.

Adjectives describe aspects of something or someone, such as what he/she/it looks like. If you get stuck for ideas, think of the five senses. What can you see? For example, what colour is it? What can you hear or feel? How does it smell or taste? It always helps a reader if they can get a sense of what it would have felt like to share the experience.

3 Use the following connective words to help you complete your writing.

- As well as this
- Then
- Similarly
- Additionally
- And
- Finally
- Alongside the
- Next to
- Another example of this

More practice . . .

4 The examiners could ask you to write a description text on any topic. Have a go at this exam-level question to perfect your technique.

 People can think very differently about places. Think of a place you know very well. It might be somewhere near home or somewhere you go on holiday. DESCRIBE the things you like about it and the things you do not like about it.

AFTER ANSWERING . . .

If you have completed all these questions, you can begin to feel confident about your skills with these objectives. Look at the checklist below and grade your skills to make sure you're ready to tackle an exam question.

Skill	I need more practice	I usually get it right	I am ready to move on
Identify my reader and purpose			
Structure my description			
Organise sentences well			
Use paragraphs effectively			
Use punctuation accurately			
Use appropriate words to describe			
Spell words correctly			

WHAT NEXT?

If you need more help with writing non-fiction texts, try quick activities 2 and 11 on pages 123 and 128.

PART ONE – UNDERSTANDING MEDIA TECHNIQUES

YOUR OBJECTIVES ARE . . .

- to think about the purpose
- to think about the intended audience
- to identify specific presentation features
- to talk about your ideas and opinions in detail
- to organise your writing clearly.

The media includes many different formats.

Internet Radio
Magazines Newspapers
ADVERTS
Television

And many more . . .

Some of these formats are covered in other parts of this book. Here we are going to focus on just one area of the media – TELEVISION. Most people are pretty familiar with the different types of TV programme, whether they are three-hour films or five-minute cartoons.

All TV shows have a DIRECTOR – the person who decides exactly what the programme is going to be like. The director might have a variety of PURPOSES when directing the show. The main purpose of most TV shows is to ENTERTAIN the audience. Think about it – if the show WASN'T entertaining, you would not watch it again!

However, you may not realise that all TV directors try to influence the viewer in a certain way and so entertain them. The director might want the audience to laugh, to feel fear, suspense, or like they are close to the person on screen, or even to make them hate a character. We tend to feel more entertained if we've felt some sort of emotion.

Directors often use certain tricks to help you feel some of these emotions to make good entertainment. Which of these tricks can you remember seeing on screen?

Feature tricks	
Lighting	Can be used to create different effects, such as spotlights to put someone under pressure or bright sunshine to suggest a happy mood.
Sound effects	Sound effects are important for suggesting mood, such as a ticking clock sound to build pressure or a crashing sound to suggest an accident without showing it.
Music	Music is also important to build atmosphere, such as soft music to build romance or hard rock to suggest a violent mood.
Special effects	Special camera tricks can be used to suggest ghostly appearances or super fast fighting speeds to show extra special action powers.
Voice over	A voice over on film is used to help tell the story of what is happening and also to make you feel closer to what the character is feeling.
Flashbacks	Moments from the past may be put next to other scenes to add drama or to add to our understanding of a character.
Opening credits	May influence what you think about the programme before it starts, for example they may be exciting or colourful.

As well as these tricks, directors can decide to use the cameras in different ways. Certain camera angles can make all the difference to the way we see a shot and what emotion we feel with it.

Camera tricks	
Long shot	Shows the scene where the action will take place.
High angle shot	Can show a character is under pressure because it makes them look small.
Medium shot	Shows some of the background and a better view of one or more characters.
Low angle shot	Shows a character or situation from below, which can make it or them seem more threatening.
Close-up	Shows the reaction of a character with their face in focus.
Big close-up	Shows a small detail in close focus, like a really close face shot to show emotion.

NOW TRY THESE ACTIVITIES . . .

1 Work out which emotions different types of TV programmes try to make you feel. Some programmes might try to make you feel more than one emotion.

Discuss your ideas with other members of your class. Use a grid like the one here to help you. Some ideas have been filled in to start you off. Add other types of programme that you are familiar with.

Type of programme	Examples you have seen	Emotions felt
Sport	Grandstand, Match of the Day	• Fear (that your team will lose) • Amazement (at the statistics) • Suspense (will Beckham get it in?)
Soap	Eastenders, Hollyoaks	• Sadness (when a character is killed off) • Happiness (at a wedding) • Shock (when someone is murdered)
Quiz show		
Game show		
Nature documentary		
News		

2 Watch 15 minutes of a drama programme. It could be part of a soap, a drama special, or even a film. Your teacher may supply a video for this task or ask you to bring one from home.

Working in a group, how many of the tricks and camera angles can you see? Take notes as you watch.

You may find it easier if you split into groups before you start and have each group looking for just a few types of trick or camera angle.

When the video is finished, discuss with the group what the PURPOSE was of each of those tricks? WHY was it used? What EMOTION did the director want you to feel?

3 The writer and director of a TV programme have to think about the audience, in the same way writers of fiction or non-fiction do.

WHO are they trying to attract to watch the show?

WHO will be entertained by the programme?

Although some shows are meant for any type of audience, many have a very specific type of audience in mind. The writer and director try to give a programme the type of contents they think a certain audience will like. For example, *Blue Peter* is produced for children of a very specific age. And have you ever heard gangsta rap in a gardening programme – no, because it does not suit what the audience would like!

Using a grid like the one below, think of the likely audience for each type of programme. The first few examples have been filled in for you.

Type of show	Likely audience
Football show	Football fans, probably more male than female; any age.
Gardening show	Male or female; probably older; gardening fans.
Quiz show	Male or female; probably adults, depending on the quiz.
Nature documentary	
News	
Cartoon	
Cookery show	
Late night comedy	

4 You may have watched TV Talk shows, such as Jerry Springer, Ricki Lake, Kilroy or Trisha. These types of shows usually have a theme or question for the day and bring in members of the public to discuss the issue.

The directors of these shows are very careful to select people who have strong feelings on the topic and who are likely to disagree. This usually makes for interesting and entertaining watching.

You could run a talk show in your own classroom, because talk shows are organised in a similar way to lessons. Think about it – there is one person in charge, telling people when they can speak and asking others what they think. At the end, the person in charge usually sums up what has been discussed. Sounds a lot like a lesson, doesn't it!

You could run the show with a small group of five or six class members. However, it may be possible to involve the whole class, which can make it very interesting.

First take some time for preparation. You'll need to decide on the following.

- Will you set up a camcorder to film the show so you can watch and discuss it later?
- Do you want your teacher or a brave member of the class to act as the show host? It's not easy!
- What is your own opinion about the topic for discussion?
- Who will be in the audience of the show? This is in school, so there can't be any bad language or fighting!
- How will guests who over react be dealt with? On TV, they are asked to leave the studio.
- How long will each person be allowed for their piece? How long will the whole show be? It's up to the host to make sure the timing runs smoothly.
- How long will the host take to introduce the topic for discussion, how they will introduce the guests, how they will deal with the audience, and how they will end the show?
- Should there be a vote at the end of the show? Should the last word be left to an expert or maybe a member of the audience should decide who is right?

5 You are going to stage a 'Ricki Lake Show.' The focus for this show is on smoking and cigarettes. Many smokers say they have a right to choose to smoke or not. But think about it – if cigarettes kill or cause disease, shouldn't people be protected, even from themselves? Should cigarettes be totally banned or not? What's your view?

Use the Director's Sheet on the next page to help you stage the show. You may want to use all or just a few of the suggested guests or make up some of your own.

It's important that everyone involved has time to prepare. Class members will need to get into character if they are playing one of the guests. Members of the audience should write questions to ask each of the guests during the show.

DIRECTOR'S SHEET

The Ricki Lake Show – At Your School

Cigarettes kill thousands of Britons every year – should they be made illegal?

We have several guests on today's show.

A government minister. She was part of the government committee that fought to outlaw tobacco advertising in magazines, newspapers and on billboards, and to put bigger health warnings on cigarette packets.

A 65-year old smoker. He's smokes 40 a day most of his life. He knows it's addictive, but he doesn't try to give up because he reckons he's as fit as a fiddle and it hasn't harmed his health.

A young mum with two small children. She was very upset when her doctor told her that because she smoked while she was pregnant, her eldest child has asthma. She's given up now, but still feels guilty when her little girl has an attack.

A 45-year old man with lung cancer. He was horrified when he found out he'd got cancer, but now he's having to learn to live with it and not being able to do the things he used to enjoy. He still feels frightened about dying in pain, though.

Editor of a leading men's health magazine. He's been running a campaign in the magazine to promote the idea that a healthy body comes from healthy living, which includes not smoking.

A 15-year old teenager who wants to smoke because all her friends do, but her dad says 'He'll kill her!' if she starts. She thinks her dad just wants to stop her having fun and making grown up decisions.

A spokesman for a smoker's organisation. She believes it is a basic human right to make one's own choices, including about whether to smoke or not. She also thinks tobacco advertising should not be banned because smokers have a right to be given information through adverts.

A leading advertising model. He believes his brief was to sell an image to young boys to attract new smokers, despite whatever the tobacco industry claims.

The manager director of a major tobacco company. He says he doesn't believe that a link between smoking and lung cancer has been properly proved. In any case, he also has to think about his workers, who would lose their jobs if cigarettes were made illegal.

Our expert today is the **psychologist, Dr Michaela Day**. She will give advice to some of our guests and answer questions from the audience.

Our final guest is **Mr Joe Bloggs** – the man on the street.

He holds the opinions of the general public – but what are they?

Today he will decide whether cigarettes should be made illegal or not, according to the strongest arguments from our guests.

It's up to the guests and the audience to convince him that what they think is right.

6 After the show, it's important to discuss as a class what you thought went well. Which guest was really in character and convinced you all? Which member of the audience asked some really difficult questions to put the guests on the spot? Was the ending successful? Did the man on the street make a decision? If not, why not? What would you do differently next time?

7 If you want to try another show or a different topic, you'll have to write your own Director's Sheet. Everyone in the class could share this task with each person writing their own character.

Here are some suggestions for show titles. The guests and final decisions are up to you.
- Extreme sports are too dangerous. Should they be banned?
- School holidays are too long. Should they be shortened?
- Should the legal age for drinking alcohol in Britain be higher?
- Beauty contests, page 3 and fashion modelling. Are they bad for the image of women?

AFTER ANSWERING . . .

Read the notes below to help you think about what you have learned.

The first three activities look at how well you've understood how directors use emotions, feature tricks and camera angles to make programmes appeal to different aiudiences.

The next three activities help you explore how a talk show is organised and help you analyse the contributions of the participants.

SUMMARY

Remember to:
- decide what emotions the show makes you feel
- think about what type of person enjoys different types of show
- look at the effects of the presentation tricks
- decide what you think about the topics raised
- plan how you will talk about your opinions.

WHAT NEXT?

You'll have the chance to use these skills more independently in the Practice section on pages 113–115.

PRACTICE – WRITING ABOUT MEDIA TEXTS

REMEMBER: the key is to think about what effects and emotions the show produces and to explain your opinions clearly and in detail.

NOW PRACTISE . . .

Now you have thought about TV audiences and staged your own show, you probably feel like sitting back and watching one instead!

You must be able to analyse media texts or write a report to show you understand the tricks they use and that you can write clearly about your opinion of them for your coursework.

Analysing talk shows

1 Watch a video of any talk show, such as the British Kilroy or Trisha or the American Jerry Springer or Oprah Winfrey. Make notes in answer to the questions below as you watch the programme. You may need to watch the video twice.

What is the programme's purpose and intended audience?
a What is the purpose of this TV show?
b What is the topic being discussed?
c Who is the intended audience? How do you know?
d Is the programme divided into sections? What are they and why do you think this is?
e What is meant to happen at the end of the show? Does it?
f Do you think the show was successful in its intentions? Why do you think that is?

How does the programme influence what you think about it?
a How long does the programme last?
b What are the opening credits of the programme like? Why do you think this is?
c Are any special lighting, music, sound, or vision effects used to influence the TV audience? How do they work?
d Are any special camera angles used to influence the TV audience? How do they work?
e How would you describe the job of the host of the show? Why do you think that person in particular was chosen?
f Would you watch the show again? If not, is that because you're not part of the intended audience?

Analysing a guest

2 Choose one guest from the show and watch the video again, focusing on just that person. Think about the following questions, writing notes to help you in your final analysis.

a What is the purpose of having this guest on the show?
b Do they seem very emotional?
c Are we meant to like them or not? Why do you think that it?
d How are they dressed? Is that meant to make us think something about them?
e Does the host of the show seem to like them?
f Now ask yourself again – what is the purpose of having them on the show?

Analysing the host

3 Watch the show again, this time focusing on the host. Think about the following questions, again making notes for your final analysis.

a What is the purpose of having this host on the show?
b Was this host famous for something else before this show? Is there a connection between what they were famous for before and what this show is about?
c Are we meant to like them or not? Why do you think that is?
d Is the way they are dressed meant to make us think something about them?
e Do the guests on the show seem to like them?
f Why do you think this person was chosen to host this show?

4 Then write up your answers to the questions as an analysis essay. Remember to write about all the points in the questions. Use as much of the frame below as fits your chosen programme to help you. Note that it uses the questions to help you structure your writing.

Analysis of a talk show

The show I watched was called '................................' and it lasted for
....

The purpose of the show was ....
The intended audience was .... I knew this because
....

The opening credits of the programme were .... I thought this was because ....

The show discussed the topic of ....

It was divided in .... main sections which dealt with .... I thought this was good/bad because ....

During the show, special effects were used to influence the TV audience. They were .... They had the effect of ....

Different camera angles were also used to influence the audience. The .... angle had the effect of ....

One of the guests on the show was particularly good/awful. He/she was .... I thought they were included on the show because ....

The job of the TV host of the show was to .... He/she was very good because he/she ....

At the end of the show .... was meant to happen. It did/didn't happen and that made a good/bad ending because ....

I think the show was very successful/unsuccessful in fulfilling its intentions. This is because ....

I enjoyed/didn't enjoy the show and would definitely watch/not watch it again. This is probably because ....

AFTER ANSWERING . . .

After you have written your essay, you can begin to feel confident about your skills with these objectives. Look at the checklist below and grade your skills to see if there is anything you need to look at again.

Skill	I need more practice	I usually get it right	I am ready to move on
Identify the purpose and intended audience			
Recognise the effects of the presentation tricks			
Organise my opinions clearly in writing			
Use sentences and punctuation carefully			
Use paragraphs effectively			
Check vocabulary and spelling carefully			

QUICK PRACTICE ACTIVITIES

In this section there are quick activities for you to practise many of the general skills for reading and writing.

You might decide after completing one of the sections in the rest of the book that you need more practice in one specific skill to give you more confidence. Here you will find some quick activities to practice that skill. On the other hand, you could refer directly to the activities here to help you revise one or more skills that you have not worked on for a while.

Part one – reading skills

1 Recognising different text forms and purposes

You are already familiar with different forms of text. You are aware that texts can be long, as in books, magazines, and leaflets, or very short, as in adverts, or on signs and notices.

Look at the six texts below. Decide where you would see each text and also the main purpose of each one. Remember, the purpose of a text can be to inform, explain, describe, argue, persuade and/or to advise. For example, we see the sign here many times in a day. We know it is a traffic sign and that it has two main purposes. It informs us that the speed limit is 30 miles per hour, but it also instructs us not to go over that speed.

a No Smoking.
b Next left for fresh farm eggs.
c Buy British.
d High tide at 06:10 today.
e Wash separately at 40 degrees.
f In an emergency, break glass.

2 Grasping the key idea and purpose in text

A The key idea in a text is the main message or purpose. What is the key idea of this non-fiction text?

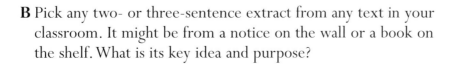

The British Red Cross cares for people in crisis at home and abroad. It gives vital support during both major emergencies and personal crises, and provides comprehensive training in First Aid and caring skills.

a To describe the work of the Red Cross.
b To persuade you to support the Red Cross.
c To advise you on how to join the Red Cross.

B Pick any two- or three-sentence extract from any text in your classroom. It might be from a notice on the wall or a book on the shelf. What is its key idea and purpose?

117

3 Understanding the characters in a text

Read this extract from *Bravo Two Zero*, a novel by Andy McNab, about soldiers on manoeuvre.

> Apart from his success with women, the most noticeable thing about Stan was his dress sense: he didn't have any. Until the squadron got hold of him, he used to go everywhere in Crimplene* safari jackets and trousers that just stopped short of his ankles. All in all a very approachable, friendly character, there was nothing that Stan couldn't take in his stride. If he hadn't been in the Regiment, he would have been a yuppie or a spy – albeit* in a Crimplene suit.
>
> *Glossary: Crimplene = unfashionable fabric; albeit = although.

Now you should have the beginnings of a picture of the type of man Stan is in your mind. Practise your skills of understanding characters by answering this question.

How do you know that Stan must be pretty successful in his career? Choose two main reasons from this list.
a The narrator says he would have had a successful job as a yuppie or a spy even if he had not been in the Regiment.
b He used to wear naff trousers that were too short for him.
c There is nothing he cannot take in his stride.
d He is successful with women.

4 Inferring and deducing from texts

Re-read the extract about Stan. You will be able to work out some things about Stan, even when the text does not put them into words. Practise these skills of inferring and deducing things from a text by answering this question.

How can you tell that the narrator likes Stan? Select three of the words or phrases from below and use them in a sentence to explain how you know this.
a 'approachable'
b 'Crimplene suit'
c 'friendly'
d 'success with women'
d 'he would have been a yuppie'
e 'nothing that Stan couldn't take in his stride'

Use the question to help you phrase your answer. For example,

I can tell that the narrator likes Stan because he uses words like ....

5 Making reference to texts to support a point

Read this extract from the sports pages of *The Sun* newspaper.

It is one of the few remaining mysteries of modern day football. How can some teams be so good in their own back yard and so awful as soon as they hit the road?

Take First Division Watford [nicknamed The Hornets by their fans], for instance, FA Cup conquerors of Premiership newcomers West Brom at Vicarage Road [their home ground].

The Hornets have won 9 league games on their own patch. They have slammed in 26 goals while conceding only 16 to give a healthy looking 'balance sheet.'

But put them on a coach, drive a few miles either up or down the M1 and it is all change. They have taken a measly 11 points from 14 games, while leaking 29 goals and scoring just NINE. ■

You should be able to choose quotes from a text to prove whatever you want to say about it. Practise your skill by answering this question.

The writer suggests that Watford play well when they are at their home ground. Choose any line or phrase from the text to put into the following sentence.

The writer shows how well Watford do at home when he says,
'...........'.

6 Gathering information from texts

Re-read the article about Watford. Can you pick out and understand small bits of information in the text? Practise your skill in gathering information from texts by answering these questions.
a How many goals have Watford scored at home this season?
   ■ 26 ■ 16 ■ 11
b How many away games have Watford played?
   ■ 11 ■ 14 ■ 29
c What is the name of Watford's home ground?

7 Express a personal opinion

Read this extract from Mike Gayle's comic novel called *My Legendary Girlfriend*. Will, the narrator, has just started work as a teacher and is telling a friend about it.

'It's horrible,' I said. 'A total nightmare. I can't coast or take it easy for a second, otherwise they'll skin me alive. I can't show any weakness. The kids, they can smell weakness from a mile off. Once they catch a whiff it sends them wild. They're like a pack of hyenas preying on a wounded antelope. Sarah, another newly qualified teacher, broke down in tears in front of a class on Thursday. I give her another week before she's looking at her careeer options.'
Alice laughed.
'It's not funny you know,' I said.
'No, of course it's not funny.'

The examiners want to know your opinion on what is happening in a text. You should be able to explain your opinion clearly. Answer the following question to practise this skill.

How do you think Will feels about his new job? Choose one or more of these words to express what you think in a sentence.
- miserable
- happy
- amused
- defeated
- confused
- worried
- stressed

8 Backing up an opinion with evidence from the text

You must be able to choose a quote from the text to prove anything that you say about it. Re-read Will's story and answer the following questions to practise this skill.

A Choose one of these quotes to explain your opinion on how Will feels. Use this sentence opener to help you.

Will feels .... I know that he feels this way because he says that, '...........'.

a 'It's horrible'
b 'A total nightmare'
c 'They'll skin me alive'

B Do you think Alice is going to be sympathetic towards Will and his problems? Which of these quotes is the best reason for what you think? Use it in a sentence to explain what you think.
a 'not funny'
b 'laughed'
c 'of course'

9 Understanding characters through dialogue

Read this extract from *Lord of the Flies*, by William Golding. Some boys are stuck on a desert island and are arguing over making shelters and catching food.

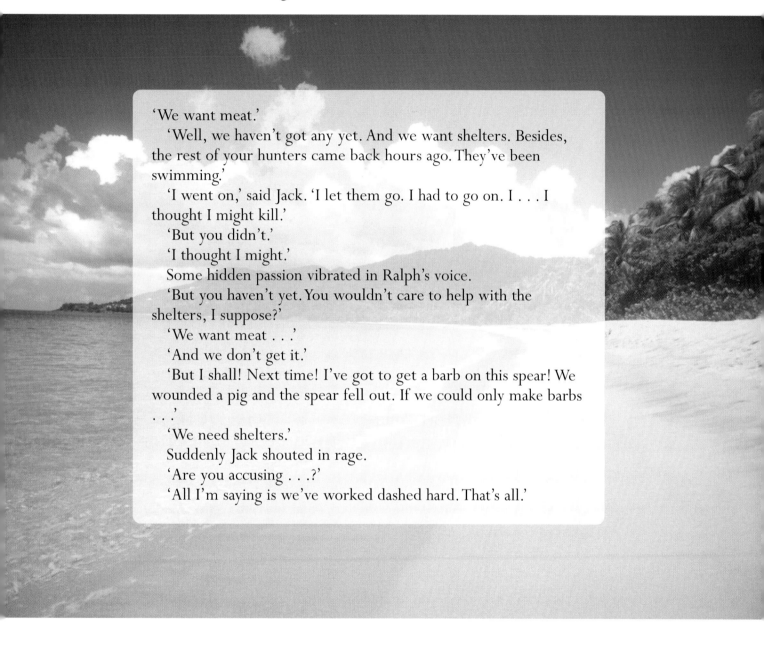

'We want meat.'

'Well, we haven't got any yet. And we want shelters. Besides, the rest of your hunters came back hours ago. They've been swimming.'

'I went on,' said Jack. 'I let them go. I had to go on. I . . . I thought I might kill.'

'But you didn't.'

'I thought I might.'

Some hidden passion vibrated in Ralph's voice.

'But you haven't yet. You wouldn't care to help with the shelters, I suppose?'

'We want meat . . .'

'And we don't get it.'

'But I shall! Next time! I've got to get a barb on this spear! We wounded a pig and the spear fell out. If we could only make barbs . . .'

'We need shelters.'

Suddenly Jack shouted in rage.

'Are you accusing . . .?'

'All I'm saying is we've worked dashed hard. That's all.'

You must be able to show that you understand how characters are shown through what they say, the dialogue. Answer the following questions to practice this skill.

Use quotes to support your answers wherever you can.

a What is really important to Ralph?

b What is Jack getting so frustrated about?

c How do you know that these two boys do not get on very well?

10 Recognising different sections

Read this extract from the *Eyewitness Travel Guide: New York*.

What To Eat In New York

The variety of food in New York is as varied as its cultural and ethnic makeup and you can find virtually any food you want. If you fancy a hearty simple meal, such as marinated vegetables, pasta or salami, visit one of the many Italian restaurants found in every neighbourhood. For a more sophisticated meal try a Japanese restaurant for sushi and sashimi – considered as good as anywhere in Japan. Or you could try some traditional Jewish foods, like pastrami, blintzes and bagels, found in most delis and luncheonettes. Spicy curries can be found in the many Indian restaurants around Manhattan. If you are really hungry, visit a steakhouse for juicy steaks, fresh seafood and some especially wicked desserts.

This extract could be split up into six different sections. The first one is the first sentence and introduces the different foods in New York. The last section is about steakhouse food. Practise recognising or classifying different sections by answering these questions.

a What are the four other sections in this extract between the first and the last ones?
b In which section is sushi mentioned?
c Although it is not mentioned specifically, in which section could you talk about chicken korma with pilau rice?

PART TWO – WRITING SKILLS

1 Writing simple chronological narrative

This is not as difficult as it sounds. It just means writing down what happened in time order. You can usually follow this structure.

- Introduce the topic.
- Work through the events, using time connectives to link your ideas and sentences.
- Write a concluding sentence to sum up.

Try one of these three examples to practise.

a Write a chronological narrative of what happened when you got up this morning.

b Write a chronological narrative of what happened in your favourite soap last night.

c Write a chronological narrative of a football match you have seen.

Use these time connective words to help you, adding more of your own.

- First
- After that
- The next morning
- Gradually

- Then
- Just then
- Suddenly
- In the end

- Next
- Hours later
- Seconds later
- Finally

2 Adapting writing to different readers

It is vital to decide on the type of audience you are writing for. You must appeal to your audience if you are to achieve your purpose.

Imagine your purpose is to persuade your audience to buy a product. It might be a drink.

A Plan an advert to sell your drink to small children. You know that kids like fruity flavours and cartoon characters. You need to think of the following.

  a A name for your drink that will appeal to your audience.

  b Something you can say about the taste of your drink to make it sound more appealing.

  c A slogan for your drink that will interest your audience.

B Design your advert and try it out to see if members of your class think it will work. Make changes to your advert if necessary.

C Try the same process for two new drinks for two new audiences, perhaps men in their 20s and 30s, and ladies over the age of 75. What will attract each of these groups?

3 Using sentences in a logical sequence

If you can work out a sensible order for the sentences you read, you can plan your own writing with the same skills.

A The sentences below are from instructions for setting the timer on a video recorder, but they've been muddled up. Use the connective words, as well as the meaning of the sentences, to help you find the correct order.

   a Next, complete the sections on date and time for the programme you wish to record.

   b Your video should now be ready to record your programme – happy watching!

   c First, select a blank tape and place in the machine.

   d Finally, select 'OK' on the remote to confirm all the details are correct and to complete programming.

   e Choose the channel that you wish to record.

   f Then select 'Menu' on your remote control to begin programming.

B Why was it easy to find which one to start with?

4 Varying vocabulary for interest

Read this very boring opening for a horror story. The author has no idea how to use descriptive vocabulary to make a story interesting.

> The .... **man walked** up to the .... **house**. He .... opened the .... door and .... **walked** inside. The floor was .... **dirty** and the walls were .... **dark**. He heard a .... **noise** upstairs, so he started to .... **climb** the .... stairs. The .... **noise** was **coming** from behind a .... **door** at the .... **end of the landing**.

A Improve the vocabulary in this boring story. Either add descriptive words in the gaps or change the words in bold for more interesting ones. For example, the first line could be improved to read:

> The scruffy looking man walked up to the deserted house.

Or even,

> The monk crept up to the asylum.

B Compare your story opening with your partner's opening to see who chose the best words.

5 Spelling words correctly

There are various ways to help you learn words that you know you often get wrong. Try using some of the following methods.

A Learn a rhyme or saying, or mnemonic, in which the first letter of each word reminds you of the letters in the word you can't remember. For example,

Never **E**at **C**hips **E**at **S**alad **S**andwiches **A**nd **R**emain **Y**oung – will remind you of NECESSARY, and

Big **E**lephants **C**an't **A**lways **U**se **S**mall **E**xits – reminds you of BECAUSE.

You can make up your own mnemonics for words you have trouble with. The more amusing, the better!

B Look for little words within the big words you need to remember how to spell. For example,
  a rat in sepa**rat**e
  b bus in **bus**iness
  c die in sol**die**r.

The words within words you choose can be your own little jokes – you'll never spell them incorrectly again.

C Use the Look–Cover–Write–Check memorising technique to fix difficult spellings in your head. Look at one particular word, cover it up and write it down, and then check if you wrote it correctly. Repeat the process 20 times and it might just stay in your head.

D Ask your teacher if there are certain spelling patterns that you keep getting wrong. It might always be words with plural endings or words with a long 'a' sound. Then you can focus on learning the rules for that type of spelling to break your mistake pattern for ever.

E Keep a spelling log of the words you get wrong most often. If you know what the enemy is, you can start to form a battle plan against it and finally defeat it. Be armed with knowledge!

6 Write simple sentences

Simple sentences are needed to give clear information to readers or to create impact in a punchy way. They have a capital letter at the beginning, a full stop at the end, have no commas, and tend not to use 'and' or 'then'.

Turn these notes for instructions on how to make a banana smoothie into a series of simple sentences.

- liquidiser
- 1 pint cold milk
- 3 tablespoons vanilla ice-cream
- drink immediately
- 2 chopped bananas
- 2 teaspoons honey
- 1 minute on full power

7 Writing complex sentences

Complex sentences are used when lots of information needs to be included in a sentence. They may use a variety of punctuation and a variety of connectives such as 'and', 'then', 'which', 'who', 'with', or 'as well as' to link clauses and ideas.

Turn these notes for a description of a burglar into a descriptive text, using complex sentences. Group all similar information into one complex sentence.

- man
- maybe 6 foot 3 inches
- short blonde hair
- slight lisp
- 'Chelsea' tattoo on left hand
- striped sides
- broad
- tall
- north London accent
- shaved up the back
- blonde goatee beard
- black tracksuit
- white trainers

8 Using full stops, capitals and question marks correctly

A full stop is needed at the end of every sentence, to show it has ended. A question mark is needed at the end of a question. Capital letters are needed:

- at the beginning of every sentence
- for the names and titles of people, e.g. Mr Homer Simpson, the Prime Minister
- for the names of places and rivers, e.g. South Africa, Norfolk Broads, River Thames
- for the names of companies and trade names, e.g. Cadbury's, Kleenex
- for named or recognised ships, aircraft, cars and bikes, e.g. the Titanic, Concorde, Golf GTI

- for the names of institutions, e.g. House of Commons, the Labour party
- for days of the week, months and special holidays, e.g. Monday, Easter, Ramadan
- for abbreviations, e.g. RSPCA.

Add capital letters and punctuation to the following six sentences.

a thierry henry originally came from france

b america's intelligence organisations include the fbi, the cia and the nsa

c why was owen dropped from the squad in april

d the world's best cymbals are made by zildjian in turkey

e why has mel gibson never made a christmas film

f ducati motorbikes are very popular in the usa

9 Using different punctuation marks

Commas are punctuation marks that are often over used. You need to be certain you are using them correctly, especially in writing that the examiners will see. Commas can be used in a sentence when:

- you want to split up items in a list, e.g.

  I've bet on numbers four, six, eight, and twelve.

- you want to separate two clauses (parts) of a sentence that relate to each other, but need a pause in between, e.g.

  The dog ran off with the sausage, which was now in a terrible state.

- you want to add an extra bit of information to the middle of a sentence, e.g.

  The man, who was covered in mud, walked into the pub.

You should NOT use commas to run lots of short sentences together. Be very clear about where a sentence ends.

Look at these WRONG examples. Use full stops, capital letters, commas and connectives to correct the sentences. Some may be better as more than one sentence or just need more commas.

a I was tired, I went to bed, this noise woke me up, I went downstairs to see what it was.

b Dougie had bought ham salami pastrami and cheese for his sandwich.

c Kevin who was absolutely shattered slept until 4pm the next day.

d He had said he would wait but he was not a patient man.

10 Writing dialogue

There are two sets of rules for writing dialogue, or speech, in a text – for setting it out correctly and for making it interesting. Dialogue must be set out with the proper punctuation.

a Always start a new line each time a new speaker starts talking.

b Include every word a person actually says inside speech marks. You DON'T put the 'he said' bit inside the speech marks.

c Make sure there's some punctuation on the inside of the last speech mark. This may be a question mark, exclamation mark, or sometimes a full stop, but is usually a comma, e.g.

'What was that?' asked Liam.
'I don't know,' replied Jazmin.

To make dialogue interesting, you must do the following.

a Make sure your characters only say what is necessary for the story. Don't let them waffle on and get boring.

b Make every line your characters say tell us about their feelings. Are they scared? Angry? Bored? You need to show that.

c Use the 'he said' bit better. Instead of 'said,' use words that show HOW your character said something.

Now have a quick practice. Write ten lines of a dialogue in which two getaway drivers are waiting outside a bank robbery. Something is going wrong, but they do not know what yet.

11 Using paragraphs

Paragraphs split different topics in the text into separate sections. If you were planning an essay, you might decide to use five paragraphs: one for an introduction, three for different types of detail, and one to conclude. For example, the plan for an essay on how to care for a dog, might look like this.

Paragraph One: Introducing dog care

Paragraph Two: Discussing food

Paragraph Three: Discussing exercise

Paragraph Four: Discussing love and attention

Paragraph Five: Conclusion to sum up

Write a short paragraph plan for each of the following texts.

a Explaining how to play any card game.

b Describing a battle scene.

c Information about computer games.